DOGFIGHT 11

Fw 190 *Sturmjäger*
Defence of the Reich 1943–45

Robert Forsyth

OSPREY PUBLISHING
Bloomsbury Publishing Plc
Kemp House, Chawley Park, Cumnor Hill, Oxford,
OX2 9PH, UK
29 Earlsfort Terrace, Dublin 2, Ireland
1385 Broadway, 5th Floor, New York, NY 10018, USA
E-mail: info@ospreypublishing.com
www.ospreypublishing.com

OSPREY is a trademark of Osprey Publishing Ltd

First published in Great Britain in 2024

A catalogue record for this book is available from the
British Library.

ISBN: PB 9781472857460; eBook 9781472857446;
ePDF 9781472857453; XML 9781472857477

24 25 26 27 28 10 9 8 7 6 5 4 3 2 1

Edited by Tony Holmes
Cover and battlescene artwork by Gareth Hector
Ribbon and tactical diagrams by Tim Brown
Armament artwork by Jim Laurier
Maps by www.bounford.com
Index by Angela Hall
Typeset by PDQ Digital Media Solutions, UK
Printed and bound in India by Replika Press Private Ltd

Osprey Publishing supports the Woodland Trust, the UK's
leading woodland conservation charity.

To find out more about our authors and books visit www.
ospreypublishing.com. Here you will find extracts, author
interviews, details of forthcoming events and the option to sign
up for our newsletter.

Front Cover Artwork: On 28 May 1944, the USAAF's Eighth
Air Force despatched 1341 bombers against oil and rail targets
in Germany. Around 500 aircraft were forced to abort due to
weather, and against the remaining balance of this force, the
Luftwaffe's I. *Jagdkorps* deployed 333 single- and twin-engined
fighters. Although 266 of the interceptors engaged the bombers,
the latter caused heavy damage to a tank depot at Magdeburg, a
sugar refinery at Dessau and three hydrogenation plants at
Leuna.

Gareth Hector's cover illustration depicts Fw 190A-8 Wk-Nr
680143 'White 9' of 4./JG 1 as its pilot, Gefreiter Walter Gehr,
pulls away from a B-17F of the 3rd Bomb Division that he has
just attacked at 7500m near Magdeburg – one of 55 bombers
attacking the target. Gehr was leading a *Schwarm* of four
Fw 190s from his *Staffel*, which had taken off on an *Alarmstart*
from their base at Störmede at 1305 hrs to intercept the Flying
Fortresses. Gehr reported, 'At 1400 hrs we obtained sight of five
Pulks of Boeing FII [sic] at 7500m, with strong fighter escort.
Carrying out a tight formation attack, at 1407 hrs I fired at a
Boeing FII in the centre of the formation. I scored hits in the
cockpit area. In addition, individual parts flew away. The
Boeing lost altitude and fell away towards the rear of the
formation. As a result of the attacking enemy fighter escort,
I was forced away and could no longer observe what happened
to the Boeing.'

Gehr, who claimed a *Herausschuss* (forcing a bomber out of
its formation), had expended 130 rounds of MG 131 machine
gun and 130 rounds of MG 151/20 cannon ammunition
during the attack. A total of 26 B-17s were lost by the Eighth
Air Force that day.

Previous Page: Six Fw 190A-7s of II.(*Sturm*)/JG 300, all fitted
with drop tanks, prepare to take off from Holzkirchen on
another sortie against USAAF heavy bombers in the late
summer of 1944. (EN Archive)

Acknowledgements – I would like to acknowledge the kind
co-operation and goodwill of the late Oscar Bösch, Richard
Franz and Willi Unger, who never failed to answer my
questions. My thanks also to Eddie Creek, as ever, and to Erik
Mombeek.

Contents

CHAPTER 1   **IN BATTLE** • 4

CHAPTER 2   **SETTING THE SCENE** • 8

CHAPTER 3   **PATH TO COMBAT** • 17

CHAPTER 4   **WEAPON OF WAR** • 24

CHAPTER 5   **ART OF WAR** • 33

CHAPTER 6   **COMBAT** • 41

AFTERMATH • 76

SELECTED SOURCES • 79

INDEX • 80

IN BATTLE

By mid-May 1944, the Allied strategic air forces waging war against Germany had all but achieved air superiority over western and southern Europe. However, the Luftwaffe fighter force, despite suffering from critical shortages in pilots and fuel (but not aircraft) was still more than capable of inflicting a significant counter-blow when handled and coordinated with tactical precision.

Such was the situation when, on 29 May, the USAAF's Eighth Air Force assembled a formidable strike force to bomb nine primary targets consisting of aircraft component and assembly plants and oil storage facilities deep within the Reich. Fifteen Combat Wings comprising 443 B-24 Liberator and 550 B-17 Flying Fortress bombers, escorted by 673 fighters drawn from no fewer than 27 groups, formed up over East Anglia in the early daylight hours. The American planners intended that this vast force of more than 1600 aircraft would make what was described as a 'double thrust approach, with one large force [the B-24s] flying up over the North Sea and another one even larger [the B-17s] crossing the Zuider Zee and headed straight for Berlin.'

From this force, the 12 bomb groups (299 B-17s) of the 1st Bomb Division (BD) were assigned components factory targets at Krzesinski, Posen, Sorau and Cottbus, and an airfield at Schneidemühl.

Shortly after 0800 hrs, in northwest Europe, the Luftwaffe wireless detection network had picked up the American force assembling over Suffolk. Its presence was relayed to the fighter control staffs of the various *Jagddivision* and *Jagdführer* responsible for the tactical direction of the German home defence *Jagdgruppen*, including the bunker of 3.*Jagddivision* at Deelen, in the Netherlands, which lay directly in the path of the southernmost incoming bomber stream.

In turn, 1.*Jagddivision* quickly relayed information on the American assembly to its component units, including the *Gruppen* of *Jagdgeschwader* (JG) 1 based on airfields around Paderborn, in North Rhine-Westphalia. At 0815 hrs, the pilots of II./JG 1, under the command of Oberleutnant Georg-Peter Eder, and their 20 Fw 190A-7s and A-8s based at Störmede, 22km to the southwest of Paderborn, were placed on 15 minutes readiness to scramble. At 1043 hrs,

the same pilots were ordered to *Sitzbereitschaft*. This meant they pulled on flying helmets and checked maps and personal equipment one last time, before clambering into the cockpits of their radial-engined Focke-Wulf fighters. Exactly 18 minutes later, the *Alarmstart* ('scramble') order was given, and 20 BMW 801 engines thundered into life.

As the B-17s of the 1st BD continued on their course eastward towards their targets, the Fw 190s, led by Eder, of II./JG 1 took off from the grass runway at Störmede and formed up with aircraft from I. and III./JG 1, before making course for Dessau. After various changes of direction, tactical control of the JG 1 formation was passed to 1.*Jagddivision* as it headed into eastern central Germany. Shortly after, at 1218 hrs, several *Pulks* (formations) of Flying Fortresses were sighted flying to the southeast over the Magdeburg area, accompanied by a strong screen of escort fighters.

The fighters of II./JG 1 adopted a climbing, parallel course to the B-17s, and at 1235 hrs, Eder, a veteran of the daylight war against the '*Viermots*' (a contraction of 'four-engines') with 20 claims against them to his name, ordered his pilots to attack the lower bombers flying to the rear and right of the enemy formation. By this stage, either the escorts reacted too late to intercept the Fw 190s as they turned into attack, or they were already engaged in combatting fighters from other *Gruppen*. Carnage would ensue for the bombers.

At 7500m in the skies over the Saxony towns of Bautzen and Görlitz, the Fw 190s swept in fast through the Flying Fortresses, making it difficult for their

Contrails stream across a cloudless sky as B-17 Flying Fortresses of the Eighth Air Force fly deep into occupied Europe on another bombing raid. They appear to be early model aircraft, as no chin turrets are visible for forward defence, nor can escort fighters be seen above the formation. From mid-1944, it was unlikely that a force of this size would not have had cover. (NARA)

gunners to track the Luftwaffe fighters, and thus fire in defence. The German pilots opened fire with their 20mm MG 151 cannon and 13mm MG 131 machine guns. Amongst the pilots to attack were Leutnant Günther Buchholz and Unteroffizier Fritz Wurl, flying Fw 190A-8s from 6./JG 1. Buchholz reported:

> During this attack I fired at the Boeing flying third from right in this *Pulk* at a range of 600m, closing to 50m. I scored hits in the fuselage and the right wing of the Boeing. Individual parts broke away. The right side of the Boeing's fuselage and both right engines immediately started to burn with dark flames. The Boeing tilted over onto its left wing and fell spinning. I was not able to observe the impact of the burning individual parts on the ground because of a thick layer of haze.

However, Buchholz's actions had been witnessed, and this became his fifth victory. Alongside Buchholz, Wurl experienced a very similar engagement as he targeted the B-17 flying next to his comrade's victim. As he closed in from 300m to 100m, he fired two bursts:

The *Gruppenkommandeur* of II./JG 1, Oberleutnant Georg-Peter Eder, led his unit into action against American bombers on 29 May 1944. He is seen here following the award of the Knight's Cross on 24 June 1944. By that time, he had been credited with 50 aerial victories, of which 21 were four-engined bombers. (EN Archive)

> I observed hits to the fuselage and to both right engines, whereupon they both caught fire, trailing dark flames. Pieces flew away from the nose and cockpit. As I pulled away towards the right, I saw how, as a result of my hits, the Boeing turned over on its left wing and spun down out of control below. I received heavy defensive fire. I could not see much more because of the thick haze.

The B-17 was Wurl's third aerial victory.

The pilots of 4. *Staffel* also made an impact. Leutnant Helmut Proff flew as wingman to the leader of the lead *Schwarm* (four aircraft) from 4./JG 1:

> I fired at the fifth Boeing to the right and low. I observed the effects of my strikes in the cockpit and to the left inner engine. As I passed through the formation I saw that the Boeing I had shot up fell away from the formation and the left inner engine was burning brightly.

But at that moment Proff's own aircraft was hit and damaged in its engine by defensive fire from the American gunners, and as a result he was unable to determine what happened to his victim, which was his first aerial success.

Feldwebel Adolf Schulz closed in and opened fire on a B-17 flying to the left of the *Pulk*. He saw pieces of the forward fuselage and wings break away, and the bomber immediately went down. He was unable to observe anything further as he was low on fuel. Fuel shortage also impeded his *Staffelkamerad*, Unteroffizier Christian Knoblauch, who fired at the outermost Flying Fortress to the right of the *Pulk*. Closing to 250m, he observed strikes on the bomber's

right wing and both its engines, as well as to the cockpit area. Both the engines began to burn and plumed black smoke. As Knoblauch flew through the *Pulk*, he saw his victim drop behind its formation, with pieces breaking away, but he was unable to spot anything more as his aircraft also ran low on fuel. The B-17 was to be Knoblauch's first combat victim.

Fw 190A-7 'Yellow 5' waits at readiness in an earth revetment at Störmede in April 1944. The aircraft is adorned with the emblem of JG 1 and has a red *Geschwader* identification band applied to its rear fuselage. (EN Archive)

Unteroffizier Helmut Mertens, also of 4./JG 1, targeted the bomber flying sixth in from the right and opened fire:

> I scored hits to the cockpit and the Boeing immediately veered away to the right. I then fired at it again, observing hits to the forward section of the fuselage and the right inner engine. The engine immediately began to burn with bright flames. The Boeing then swerved to the right out of its formation. I was unable to make any further observation, as because of a shortage of fuel I had to land.

Mertens was credited with shooting down the bomber for his first victory.

Altogether, following a single one-minute pass, II./JG 1 claimed nine B-17s downed from a total of 32 bombers lost by the Eighth Air Force that day. Nine escort fighters were also lost. In a post-mission report, the Americans stated that, in fact, eight B-17s of the force which attacked Krzesinski, Posen, Sorau and Cottbus had been lost, with five of them falling to Luftwaffe fighters. Some 97 Flying Fortresses had sustained minor battle damage and five major damage (figures which included damage from Flak). The attacks by Luftwaffe fighters were deemed to have been 'not particularly aggressive'.

As a measure of the intensity of the aerial combat that took place on 28 May, for the Luftwaffe, the balance sheet was not favourable – 22 pilots killed and ten wounded and 39 aircraft lost and a further 14 damaged. This was a typical day for the Luftwaffe's home defence Fw 190 pilots.

CHAPTER 2
SETTING THE SCENE

In their official history of the USAAF in World War II, Professors Wesley F. Craven and James L. Cate write that, 'The true mission of the Eighth Air Force was to weaken Germany by hitting directly at its war potential – industrial, military and moral – although this required the previous destruction of German air power.'

The 'destruction of German air power' is a subject that has been assessed from many perspectives – historical, personal and technical – and it has filled countless books. The narrative has been to portray this initiative as a 'David and Goliath' struggle; a kind of reversal of the early years of the war when the superiority of German air power was used to bludgeon its opponents

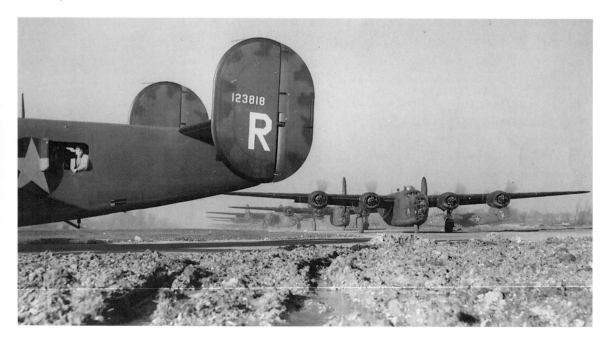

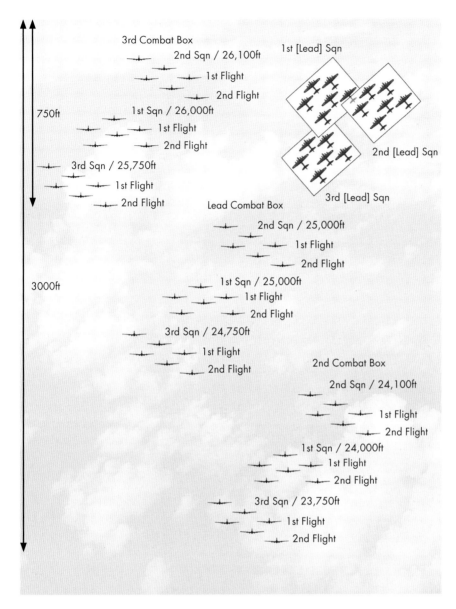

3rd Combat Box
2nd Sqn / 26,100ft
1st Flight
2nd Flight

750ft

1st Sqn / 26,000ft
1st Flight
2nd Flight

3rd Sqn / 25,750ft
1st Flight
2nd Flight

1st [Lead] Sqn

2nd [Lead] Sqn

3rd [Lead] Sqn

Lead Combat Box
2nd Sqn / 25,000ft
1st Flight
2nd Flight

3000ft

1st Sqn / 25,000ft
1st Flight
2nd Flight

3rd Sqn / 24,750ft
1st Flight
2nd Flight

2nd Combat Box
2nd Sqn / 24,100ft
1st Flight
2nd Flight

1st Sqn / 24,000ft
1st Flight
2nd Flight

3rd Sqn / 23,750ft
1st Flight
2nd Flight

The standard USAAF Combat Wing formation fielded 54 B-17s (sometimes mixed with B-24s) in three 'boxes' of bombers (in High, Lead and Low positions), each consisting of three six-aircraft squadrons echeloned into Lead, High (3rd Combat Box) and Low (2nd Combat Box). In turn, the squadrons were formed of two three-aircraft flights (High and Low). Such a formation, despite requiring considerable assembly time and disciplined flight control, ensured a high level of mutual protection and defence, although the bombers flying in the second flights of the Low squadrons were most vulnerable – they were a favourite target for rear-mounted attacks by German interceptors. Nevertheless, attacking such a formation – even without the presence of a strong fighter escort – was a daunting prospect.

and advance Hitler's war aims. But to those pilots engaged in defending the skies over the Reich in early 1944, that must have seemed a very distant and unreal memory.

The 'Goliath' facing the Luftwaffe's daylight fighter *Gruppen* by this time was the Eighth Air Force. This powerful force had arrived in Britain in the spring of 1942 and commenced operations from airfields in the country's eastern counties in August of that year. By the turn of 1943, 30 bomber missions had been flown, during which maritime, industrial, transport and airfield targets had been attacked in occupied France and the Low Countries. The Eighth's VIII Bomber Command learned lessons from these early efforts, and was progressively reinforced and expanded so that it fielded four B-17 groups and two equipped with B-24s. The commander of VIII Bomber Command,

A P-47 Thunderbolt flies close to a formation of B-17s. The appearance of such escort fighters from May 1943 made a hard job harder for the pilots of the Luftwaffe's fighter *Gruppen* defending the west and the airspace of the Reich. From then until war's end, the Luftwaffe's force strength was effectively weakened by having to separate the tactical roles of anti-bomber 'assault' fighters and high cover fighters to tackle the American escorts. (NARA)

Brig Gen Ira C. Eaker, confidently wrote in a letter to Prime Minister Winston Churchill that 'by bombing the devils around the clock, we can prevent the German defenses from getting any rest.'

And so it was that during 1943 the strategic air war waged against Germany intensified, with the number of missions increasing and target selection becoming ever bolder and deeper into Reich airspace. Improvements were made to Eighth Air Force bombing formations that saw B-17s flying in more concentrated and organised 'Combat Wings' which optimised defence against fighter attack. In May, P-47 Thunderbolts began accompanying the bombers, signalling the commencement of a massive fighter escort programme that would eventually see P-51 Mustangs flying all the way to Berlin.

However, whilst the USAAF did inflict increasingly costly and disruptive damage to German cities and factories in the first eight months of 1943, the Luftwaffe's regional commanders had devised an elastic system of defence in depth whereby most of their fighter units were held back deep in the Reich, and thus out of range of the American escorts. This meant that by the summer, some 800 single-engined fighters of the *Jagdgruppen* could be activated when needed, and then directed towards an enemy incursion by a sophisticated alert, tracking, control and radio network after the escort fighters had been forced to turn back for home due to a lack of fuel.

On 17 August 1943, the anniversary of its first heavy raid over northern Europe, VIII Bomber Command launched an attack against the ball-bearing centre of Schweinfurt. Sixty B-17s were shot down and 168 damaged. The destruction inflicted upon the factories did not compensate for the loss of more than 600 Allied airmen – especially so when the truth was that production was interrupted for only a few weeks. Indeed, German fighter production had been increasing steadily throughout the first seven months of 1943.

Over Schweinfurt, the German fighter force was able to celebrate a cautious victory, despite the fact that the losses for all participating *Geschwader* amounted to 17 pilots killed and 14 wounded, with 42 aircraft lost. The losses incurred that day included Major Wilhelm-Ferdinand 'Wutz' Galland, *Kommandeur* of II./JG 26, a respected formation leader who had 55 victories to his credit, including eight bombers. He was the brother of Generalmajor Adolf Galland, the commander of the Luftwaffe fighter arm.

Adolf Hitler welcomes Oberstleutnant Adolf Galland, the *Kommodore* of JG 26, to his headquarters on 1 July 1941 upon Galland's award of the Swords to his Knight's Cross with Oak Leaves. A little over five months later, Galland would be promoted to Oberst and appointed as commander of the Luftwaffe fighter arm. It was a task which he found challenging. Also seen here, to Hitler's left, is Generalfeldmarschall Erhard Milch, the Generalluftzeugmeister, while behind Galland is Generalfeldmarschall Wilhelm Keitel, Chief of the OKW, and at far right is General Hans Jeschonnek, Chief of the Luftwaffe General Staff. (Author's Collection)

By October the bombing campaign had reached its peak, forcing the Americans to accept that unescorted, deep penetration formations were very vulnerable. Yet though the losses incurred during such missions reached unacceptable levels, they nevertheless forced the Luftwaffe into the air to fight, and in doing so they inflicted pilot attrition on a scale from which the Germans would find it difficult to recover.

Galland reasoned that it would be prudent to limit the number of machines and operations flown by the home defence units against individual enemy raids so as to allow sufficient repair and re-grouping of aircraft which had landed on emergency fields. Only by carefully conserving strength and by efficient management of its most precious resource, namely its pilots, could the German fighter force hope to cause any damage to the bombers. This did not satisfy the Commander-in-Chief of the Luftwaffe, Reichsmarschall Hermann Göring, who insisted that all available units be thrown against every raid wherever and whenever possible. As a priority, Göring also wanted, understandably, the weight of effort directed against enemy four-engined bombers. The twin-engined *Zerstörergeschwader*, comprising Bf 110 and the new Me 410 fighters, were ordered to attack unescorted bombers, and at the same time, instructions were issued that the equipping of certain units with 21cm underwing air-to-air mortars was to be stepped up.

On 4 October, 155 B-17s, with strong P-47 escort, were assigned the industrial regions of Frankfurt and Wiesbaden, as well as the city of Frankfurt itself, as their targets. Towards 1100 hrs, Fw 190s of II./JG 1 intercepted and attacked a group of about 100 B-17s at an altitude of 8000m over the Eifel/ Wiesbaden area. Their first attack was from behind and at an angle, and was mounted without success. Four Focke-Wulfs were damaged by the defensive fire. While the *Gruppe* was reorganising itself for a second pass, it was joined by

B-17F 42-3352 *VIRGIN'S DELIGHT* from the 410th BS/94th BG passes over the Focke-Wulf assembly plant at Marienburg, in Pomerania, following its bombing run on 9 October 1943. Flying Fortresses dropped gasoline incendiary bombs for the first time on this mission. Note the factory airfield runway to the left of the smoke generated by the burning plant. Marienburg was a major centre of Fw 190 production. (NARA)

pilots from I./JG 1. During the attack four more Fw 190s were hit, but eight B-17s were shot down.

Oberleutnant Rudolf Engleder, the *Staffelkapitän* of 1./JG 1, recalled that day:

A tough encounter unfolded at an altitude of 9000–10,000m. Once again, the imposing American fighter escort engaged us in a cloudless sky. The bombardment no doubt hit the Hanau industries hard, because those responsible for its defence and the Gauleiter of Frankfurt visited Göring and protested strongly about his fighters: 'How is it possible that American bombers can fly over the city in almost parade ground fashion? And further, German fighters were seen at altitude, not attacking!' Göring went into one of his mad rages in which he thought he knew the answer, and he despatched the following orders to all the fighter units responsible:

1.   There are no meteorological conditions which will prevent fighters from taking off and engaging in combat.

2.   Every fighter pilot who lands in a machine not showing any sign of combat, or without having recorded a victory, will be prosecuted by a court-martial.

3.   In a case where a pilot uses up his ammunition, or if his weapons are unusable, he should ram the enemy bomber.

On 14 October, 229 B-17s went to Schweinfurt again. Because of fog, just two fighter groups were able to undertake escort for the B-17s. Later, as the weather cleared, the Luftwaffe committed all of its daylight fighter units, drawn from five fighter divisions – a total of 567 machines, as well as twin-engined *Zerstörer* and some fighter training school aircraft and nightfighters.

Just after 1330 hrs, as the escort began to turn back, the Fw 190s of I. and II./JG 1 dropped their auxiliary fuel tanks and turned to engage the American formation as it approached Eindhoven, attacking from '12 o'clock high' and almost immediately drawing in the fighter escort. A swirling, confused melee developed as the Germans took on both the US fighters and bombers. Oberfeldwebel Detlef Lüth claimed a B-17 for his 35th victory, while Hauptmann Emil-Rudolf Schnoor, *Kommandeur* of I./JG 1, shot down a B-17 for his 13th victory. Oberleutnant Engleder also downed one B-17 and claimed a *Herausschuss*, resulting in a personal tally of seven *Viermots* shot down or damaged in 15 days. JG 1 would end the day with total claims of 21 B-17s.

By the time the 1st BD entered the target area, it had lost 36 bombers, with one group alone losing just under half its strength. When the mission was over, the Division's loss rate had increased to 45 machines. One Combat Wing of 37 aircraft had lost 21 bombers. German losses were 31 aircraft destroyed, 12 written off and 34 damaged – between 3.4 and 4 per cent of available fighter strength in the West. One senior German air commander recorded 'the units of the German *Reichsverteidigung* [Home Air Defence] achieved a great defensive success on 14 October 1943.' For the Americans, the second Schweinfurt raid had cost VIII Bomber Command another 59 B-17s and nearly 600 aircrew. Seventeen more bombers were seriously damaged and a further 121 were damaged but repairable.

Certainly, the losses from Schweinfurt forced a halt in the progressive American strategy of hitting deep penetration targets until such time that greater numbers of long-range escort fighters were available, and so missions were kept within range of their escorts. Although it could not be said by any means that the Luftwaffe was *winning* the battle for air superiority over Europe, it was nevertheless preventing the USAAF from doing so. Equally, however, on the German side, with 67 per cent of production at Schweinfurt knocked out, the ball-bearing industry was forced to disperse its manufacturing capacity, which, in turn, presented logistics problems.

As if the increasingly regular appearance of P-47s was not enough, another ominous event occurred on 5 December with the feared debut of P-51B Mustangs of the 354th Fighter Group (FG) escorting bombers to Amiens. This would herald a new and forbidding dimension to the air war. The appearance for the first time of the Mustang caused German fighter commanders considerable concern, and forced a reappraisal of existing tactical methods. This high-powered fighter more than exceeded the speed and manoeuvrability of both the rugged, radial-engined Fw 190 and the regularly re-worked Bf 109, and was responsible for the downing of more than 70 valuable *Jagdflieger* in just two days at the end of January 1944. On 11 December, in an even more

The tense-looking pilot of a Bf 109G-6 of II./JG 2 sits close to his machine together with a group of mechanics and armourers at Evreux, in northwest France, in the autumn of 1943. The pilot wears a life jacket in readiness for immediate over-water operations, while one of the groundcrew attends to the leading edge of the wing. The Messerschmitt is fitted with a pod beneath each wing housing a single 20mm MG 151/20 cannon. In this configuration the Bf 109G-6 was known as a *'Kanonenboot'*. (EN Archive)

Line of defence. The Luftwaffe deployed its *Sturmgruppen* in a 'wall' of airfields stretching across central Germany, close to the main industrial targets and in the direct path of bomber incursions approaching from England. From these bases, they would have time to assemble into *Gefechtsverband* strength in order to engage the bombers *en masse*.

worrying development, 44 of the nimble P-51s had shielded 523 bombers all the way to Emden, in Germany.

What 1943 had exposed was the inadequacy and shortcomings in German fighter pilot training. Generally, Allied pilots benefited from far more extensive and graduated training than did their German counterparts. Reductions in the fighter training programme in the autumn of 1943 meant that replacement pilots were reaching operational units with an average of 148 hours on powered aircraft.

This state of affairs simply exacerbated the situation facing the German defence. On or around 29 December, Generalleutnant Josef Schmid, commander of I. *Jagdkorps*, which played a key role directing the fighter defence over the Reich, issued a directive to his *Jagddivision* commanders which can be seen as a harbinger of the scale of air fighting that was foreseen to be necessary to meet the Allied daylight threat. In the directive Schmid wrote:

> In view of our numerical inferiority in operations against the American attacks, it will be necessary to concentrate our units for an attack relative to time and space. Fighter attacks should be conducted in such a manner that cohesive units of the strength of at least one fighter *Geschwader* attack the bomber stream at a specific spot. By applying this method it must be possible to destroy an American bomber unit completely.

While this policy of meeting mass with mass may have been justified, the reality was that January 1944 saw the Luftwaffe suffer a 30.3 per cent loss in single-engined fighters and 16.9 per cent of its fighter pilots. With poor weather over western Europe that month Schmid further noted:

> The technical deficiencies of German fighter aircraft and the low training standard of replacement fighter pilots precluded steadily successful and effective combat against American superiority at high-altitude. Thus, January 1944 was again characterised by the inability of German forces to provide an effective defence against American daylight attacks on the Reich, let alone prevent them. Only the utmost caution in employing aircraft in bad weather – especially when take-off and landing conditions were uncertain – was able to keep German losses within reasonable limits.

In a typical such scene, pilots of 3./JG 11 sit at cockpit readiness in their Fw 190s at Husum, in northern Germany, in the early autumn of 1943. Timber taxiways have been laid over the damp ground and earth-walled blast shelters with canvas roofs can be seen in the background. (EN Archive)

In a stark indication of the attrition being inflicted, the beginning of the year also showed a percentage decrease in the Luftwaffe's Order of Battle for Bf 109 and Fw 190 interceptors from 31 per cent in 1943 to 27 per cent. By comparison, the Eighth Air Force, whose personnel numbered around 200,000, was able to recover from even heavy blows such as Schweinfurt. By early 1944 the Eighth Air Force's bomber and fighter groups were spread across more than 60 airfields in eastern England. It was able to despatch in excess of 1000 bombers and hundreds of escort fighters in one mission to northwest Europe, and by the middle of the year, the figure for bomber commitment had doubled, while 1000 fighters could be called upon for escort.

On the first day of 1944, Lt Gen Henry 'Hap' Arnold, the Commanding General of the USAAF, sent a simple message to his commanders in Europe to welcome the New Year:

> Destroy the enemy air force wherever you find them; in the air, on the ground, and in the factories.

So it was that despite bad weather conditions prevailing in Europe, January 1944 marked the beginning of an escalation in the USAAF's offensive action. Furthermore, American production and numbers of fighters and bombers reaching Europe was now literally swamping the Luftwaffe. The only major visual USAAF operation that month occurred on 11 January when the weather was expected to be fine. Conditions, however, were to prove fickle, and the American bomber force of 663 aircraft pushed on in deteriorating weather to strike at several aviation and industrial targets in the heart of the Reich, including Oschersleben, Halberstadt, Braunschweig and Osnabrück, on a mission which was to mark the commencement of Operation *Pointblank* – the strategic air offensive against Germany designed to bring about 'the progressive destruction and dislocation of the German military and economic system.' This aim was aided from the south by the USAAF's Fifteenth Air Force, which began to attack targets in Austria and southern Germany.

On 30 January newly promoted Generalmajor Schmid chaired a conference at an outpost of I. *Jagdkorps* at De Breul, in the Netherlands. Present were Generalmajor Galland and the commanders of 1., 2. and 3. *Jagddivisionen*. Schmid informed the attendees:

> The numerical strength of the American air forces in Great Britain has increased. We must face the fact that American offensive activity against the Reich will probably become greater during the coming weeks and months, and that American fighter escort will become much stronger than at present. The estimated flight range of the Thunderbolt as far as Braunschweig has not yet been confirmed. On the other hand, we know that Lightnings, equipped with auxiliary fuel tanks, are able to provide a protective screen for the bombers as far as central Germany. It is extremely important that our high-altitude fighter units provoke the Lightnings to engage in combat, so that they will be forced to dump their auxiliary tanks. If they can be forced to do so, they will have no alternative but to break off combat and return to base before running out of fuel. It does not seem likely that American fighters will be able to penetrate as far as Berlin at present.

One Fw 190 pilot, Leutnant Richard Franz of *Sturmstaffel* 1, recalled of this time:

> Although the Allies had gained air superiority in 1943, I think that the morale of our fighter pilots was not bad, especially when it is realised that the young pilots we had in the frontline units had very little experience and a life expectation of something like ten missions. It was a hard time for both the young pilots and their leaders.

And it was about to get harder. In February, the Eighth Air Force launched Operation *Argument*, or 'Big Week' – a concerted and intense bombing campaign against German aircraft production centres commencing on the 20th, specifically against the principal airframe, final assembly and component plants responsible for the output of single- and twin-engined fighter aircraft such as those at Leipzig-Mockau, Halberstadt and Regensburg. The offensive was intended to do three things – destroy German aircraft on the ground, the means of replacing them and force Luftwaffe fighters into the air to defend against the attacks, during which their fates would be sealed. This was the scenario facing the Fw 190 fighter units at the beginning of a year that would see some of the most bitterly contested aerial combat of World War II.

CHAPTER 3
PATH TO COMBAT

As has been recounted in Chapter 2, by 1943 the system of training fighter pilots in the Luftwaffe had been placed under considerable strain due to shortages in dedicated aircraft and attrition replacements, instructors, fuel and parts, not to mention increasing disruption from Allied bombing. Nevertheless, the basic process of training had remained the same since the pre-war period, even if the nomenclature used for, and within, the system underwent periodic review and change.

The career of one young man from Warstein, in Westphalia, Willi Unger, from a flight-besotted boy to an Fw 190 *Sturmgruppe* pilot typifies the training experienced by aspiring aviators. In 1934, Unger had joined his local 'Flying Hitler Youth', where he was taught how to build and fly an elementary plywood SG 38 glider. Sufficiently competent, Unger set about obtaining the required three grades of the Civil Gliding Proficiency Badge (A, B and C) over the next five years at the controls of a Grunau Baby glider. This involved five flights of 20 seconds each and one of 30 seconds (for A), five straight and level flights of 60 seconds (for B) and a final series of more lengthy flights (for C).

In October 1939, following the outbreak of war with Poland, Unger – by now a trained machine fitter – was posted to one of the many *Fliegerausbildungsregiment* (Flying Training Regiment) where future aircrew underwent a 12-month course which comprised physical fitness training and 'culture', military discipline, routine medical examinations, basic infantry training, lectures on radio and communications, map reading and orienteering, aircraft recognition and sport.

However, as Unger recalled:

At the beginning of the war, I was recruited into the Luftwaffe as a volunteer, but because of my profession as a machine fitter, I was assigned as an aircraft mechanic and not as a pilot – which is what I

One-time glider pilot Oberfeldwebel Willi Unger in typical late-war flying garb. His leather flying jacket is adorned with the 'whites of the eyes' symbols as worn by a small number of *Sturmgruppe* pilots to denote the close-range nature of their work. After a training period lasting some two years, Unger was posted from 2./*Ergänzungsjagdgruppe Ost* to IV./JG 3. With that *Gruppe* he would go on to enjoy considerable success flying the Fw 190 against USAAF bombers. (EN Archive)

wanted to be! In spite of many applications, I managed only to become a pilot at the end of 1942.

After a frustrating delay at a technical school, Unger was finally posted to the *Flugzeugführerschule* (Pilot School – FFS) A/B *Schule* No. 10 at Warnemünde on the Baltic Coast, where student pilots would undertake courses to qualify for their powered aircraft certificates. Unger embarked on his basic pilot's training in aerobatics, instrument training, formation flying and cross-country, making his first take-off on 14 December 1942.

Between 1939 and 1942, some 1100 pupils per month passed through such schools. In addition to further glider training, these schools used a variety of powered types including the Kl 35, Fw 44, Fw 58, Bü 131, Bü 181, He 51, Ar 96, Caudron C445 and the Ju W34. An initial instruction known as the '*Motor Auswahl*' (Powered Flight Selection) served to assess a pupil's performance, and to decide at an early stage whether he would be more suitable as a bomber or fighter pilot or whether further training was futile.

At *Flugzeugführerschule*, the student pilot would undertake a course to qualify for his powered aircraft certificates. The basic powered aircraft A1 certificate required that the trainee complete a loop, three landings without an error, an altitude flight to 2000m and a 300km triangular flight course. All of these were to be accomplished in one- or two-seat aircraft weighing up to 500kg. The award of an A1 certificate would mean that the student had undergone basic practical flying training in dual-control aircraft, with his instructors having taught him to take off and land, recover from a stall and be able to make basic solo flights in the vicinity of the airfield.

A2 certification was similar except that it was for aircraft with at least two seats. As most pilots in the Luftwaffe trained on dual-control machines, this was the usual starter qualification. The trainee was required to learn the theory of flight, including aerodynamics, meteorology, flying procedures and aviation law. The practical application of aeronautical engineering, elementary navigation and radio procedure was also studied.

In the air the student undertook solo cross-country flights, the duration of which was successively lengthened, and the flying of larger aircraft was practised. An element of aerobatic flying was also incorporated into the course. These licences were normally gained over a six- to ninth-month period. Initially, each instructor was assigned four pilots, but this was increased to six by 1942.

Following on from this was the B1 certificate, for which pilots progressed onto high-performance and twin-engined aircraft usually fitted with retractable undercarriages. If the pilot was assigned to fly fighters, he would then transfer to obsolescent types such as the Bf 109B/D. To obtain this certificate, the student had to show that he had already achieved at least 3000km of flight experience, flown a 600km triangular course in nine hours, an altitude flight to 4500m and at least 50 flights in aircraft in the B1 category (single-engined one-, two- or three-seaters with a maximum weight of 2500kg). On top of this experience, the pilot had to carry out three precision landings, two night landings and a night flight of at least 30 minutes.

The B2 certificate was progressively more difficult, requiring 6000km of flight experience, including at least 3000km on B1 class aircraft. In addition,

50 further night flights were necessary, which had to include several difficult night landings.

Following some 140 hours of instruction, the pupil would be given his Führerschein (Pilot's Badge), after which, as in Willi Unger's case, he would be posted to a *Jagdfliegerschule* (Fighter School). By late 1942, several *Jagdfliegerschulen* had been formed, and as new Fw 190s were delivered to operational units, older models began to become available to these training schools.

However, due to the steadily increasing rates of attrition being sustained by the Luftwaffe by the spring of 1943, the *Jagdfliegerschulen* were redesignated as *Jagdgeschwader*. JFS 1 at Werneuchen, for example, became JG 101, where the average duration of the fighter training course was three-and-a-half to four months, compared to an average of four to five months in 1942.

The instructors at the *Jagdfliegerschulen* were often highly experienced, combat-seasoned fighter pilots who had been wounded or declared unfit for operational duties due to illness. These pilots, who would have flown the Bf 109 or Fw 190 in the frontline, were invaluable. A typical example was Feldwebel Rudolf Nielinger, who had completed no fewer than 506 combat missions between 22 April 1941 and 29 January 1944 on all the main battlefronts. Nielinger was credited with 20 aerial victories flying Bf 109s with JG 51, but in January 1944 he succumbed to sandfly fever and was moved from Italy, where he had been flying combat missions over the Anzio beachhead, back to Germany, where he underwent a period of hospitalisation.

Although not fully recovered, Nielinger was posted to JG 103 on the Baltic coast in March 1944, where his flying experience was much needed and put to good use. Here, he trained new fighter pilots using a large assortment of aircraft

The relatively rare Fw 190A-5 Wk-Nr 410011 GG+MV, which was converted into a two-seat trainer at Altenburg in the autumn of 1943. Overseen by the RLM and Focke-Wulf, the conversion process was reasonably easy, with the heaviest modification work required for the centre of the fuselage. Most components were standard parts. After successful testing, the RLM ordered that ten such trainers should be built per month using A-8 airframes and the sub-designation U1. (EN Archive)

including ageing Bf 109Es and the more modern Fw 190, which included the rare A-8/U1 two-seater training variant. He ended the war flying the Me 262 in combat with JV 44.

For his part, Willi Unger was posted to 1./JG 104 at Fürth-Herzogenaurach under Oberleutnant Josef Unterberger. This *Staffel* was one of three forming the '*Geschwader*', with 2. and 3. *Staffeln* at Fürth. 1. *Staffel* formed the *Vorschule* (Preliminary School), while 2. and 3./JG 104 formed the *Endschule* (Advanced School).

Training at the *Vorschule*-level involved circuits and bumps, spot landings, turns, aerobatics, long-distance flying, navigation, diving, formation flying and some minimal awareness of battle formations and blind-flying – altogether expected to last approximately 25 hours, and conducted on the same type of aircraft as used by the A/B schools. The task of the *Endschule* was to prepare and convert the pupil onto either the Bf 109 or Fw 190 in a series of circuits and bumps in duel-control aircraft. This was followed by ten solo flights, then formation practice in pairs and fours, followed by a high-altitude flight with oxygen, a practice flight concentrating on weak points and, finally, two firing training flights, each comprising three approaches to a ground target. This covered another 16–18 hours.

Reductions in the training programme meant that by the autumn of 1943, fighter pilots were reaching their operational units with an average of 148 hours

on powered aircraft spread across an elementary A/B school, a *Jagdfliegerschule,* and an *Ergänzungsjagdgruppe* (Operational Fighter Training 'Pool'), compared to an average of 210 hours the previous year.

For potential Fw 190 pilots in 1943–44, the most common aircraft used for training were the Ar 68 and He 51 biplanes (relatively rare by 1944), the Ar 96, Bf 109D or E and captured French Dewoitine D.520s.

In June 1943, the four component *Staffeln* of *Ergänzungsjagdgruppe West* spread across southwestern France supplied Bf 109- and Fw 190-ready pilots to operational *Jagdgruppen.* Pupils were instructed by operationally-experienced instructors over courses lasting normally one month, although demands from the operational units often shortened this period to 14 days. Courses consisted of circuits and bumps in a Bf 108, prior to conversion to the Fw 190. Instruction in formation flying was similar to that received in a *Jagdfliegerschule,* but in an *Ergänzungsjagdgruppe,* at least one flight was made in a formation of seven to nine aircraft led by an instructor. Heavy emphasis was placed on gunnery training and target practice, using both machine guns and cannon.

Following two months in France with 2./*Ergänzungsjagdgruppe Ost* at La Leu, near Rochelle, in January–February 1944, Willi Unger was finally posted to his operational unit, 11./JG 3 (the *Geschwader* with which he would fly both the Bf 109G-6 and Fw 190A-8 in combat), on 10 March 1944. However, from this point on, an increasing Allied campaign of low-level attacks on German airfields, a resulting state of alert and a general feeling of insecurity badly interrupted training at all levels. During April–May 1944, 67 Luftwaffe aircraft were shot down during training, transfer or travel flights over Reich territory.

As the economic and military infrastructure of the Reich became directly threatened by the burgeoning Allied air offensive, Generalmajor Schmid, commander of I. *Jagdkorps* which controlled day fighter tactical deployment in the *Reichsverteidigung*, described the condition of the *Jagdwaffe* at this time:

Groundcrew make pre-flight checks on what is believed to be an Fw 190A-8 from 1. *Staffel* of the fighter training *Geschwader* JG 110 at Altenburg in the autumn of 1944. This *Staffel* was led by Hauptmann Willi Althof until 10 October 1944, at which point he was succeeded by Hauptmann Lorenz Göll. It appears as if a groundcrewman is assisting the pilot of the aircraft. JG 110 was formed at Altenburg on 15 October 1943, with Oberst Max Gerstenberger in command. (EN Archive)

Wooden models were used to train Luftwaffe pilots in the tactics of attacking American bombers. Here, an Fw 190 is seen making an (unlikely) high rear approach on a B-17, with the cones of fire from the bomber's defensive gun positions represented by wire. Note the positions of the wing fuel tanks have also been highlighted. (EN Archive)

Heavy losses, as well as the great physical and psychological strain imposed on German fighter pilots, reduced the combat value of our units in April and May 1944. The young replacements showed deficiencies in flying and radio usage. They lacked combat experience, particularly in respect to high-altitude operations. Time and opportunities for training in the operational units was lacking to an increasing extent. The shortage of qualified formation leaders increased. The excessive strain caused by almost uninterrupted commitment resulted in combat fatigue. Experienced fighter pilots reached the limit of their efficiency.

For Willi Unger, and hundreds of other freshly qualified fighter pilots, it was merely a portent of things to come.

Personal experiences often provided a strong motive or impetus during training. Nineteen-year-old Feldwebel Oscar Bösch, an Austrian, arrived at JG 101's base at Nancy in July 1943 for advanced training on the Bf 109. He had been posted there after completing his training at the FFS A/B 118 at Stettin. He recalled:

I must have correctly done what was needed because my transfer to the *Ergänzungsgruppe Süd* at Avignon, in southern France, came in February 1944, where I was assigned to undertake high-altitude fighter training on the Bf 109F and G-6.

This being completed, in April 1944 Bösch was posted to IV./JG 3 at Salzwedel, but on the 15th, during his journey by road to join his new unit, an incident took place in the Ruhr city of Hamm which jolted Bösch into adopting a new direction:

We stopped over in Hamm. I was there with three other pilots from my training unit and we had driven up from Avignon. It was good to be back in Germany, but I got a sudden taste of what it was like to live under heavy aerial bombardment. The American bombers came from the east and their bombs rained down close to the main railway station. It was the first major attack on Hamm. There was total panic. I had to rush down into a basement with terrorised women and children. I spent a few hours down there in the dark and the dust, listening to the bombs falling above our heads. When the first bombs landed, the lights in the cellar went out. They lit candles for light. Children cried. I had never been so frightened.

When we got out of there, the town was nothing but fire and ruins – a place like Hell. Eighty per cent of the town centre was destroyed. Later that night the RAF came and they bombed the same area. Then they came again and again. I felt so inadequate. I asked myself, 'Is it really possible that human beings could do this to one another?'

Of his training, Feldwebel Oscar Bösch commented, 'I must have correctly done what was needed'. Flying the Fw 190A-8 with *Sturmstaffel* 1 and IV./JG 3, his operational career was given some incentive after experiencing at first-hand a USAAF bombing raid on Hamm. 'When we got out of there, the city was nothing but fire and ruins.' (Author's Collection courtesy of Oscar Bösch)

It was providential that based at Salzwedel at that time was a specialist fighter unit known as *Sturmstaffel* 1, which was carrying out formative missions intended to devise more established anti-bomber tactics deploying heavily armed and armoured Fw 190s (see Chapter 5). Bösch decided to volunteer:

On 28 April, if I remember correctly, I arrived early at Salzwedel airfield. I did not have time to admire the scenery. Instead, I was 'introduced' to my Fw 190A-7, a 'pure-bred' and a massive machine. A fellow pilot explained all the refinements before letting me off on a flight, as I'd never flown one before. Everything went fine. I made four flights before taking the aircraft back to the hangar. My initial 'contact' had lasted minutes. The fifth flight took place the following morning, 29 April. It was serious that time.

CHAPTER 4
WEAPON OF WAR

The earliest incarnation of the Fw 190 fighter as a dedicated bomber attack aircraft was the A-6 variant, which had originally been the sub-variant designation for a planned ground-attack version of the Focke-Wulf. This eventually became the F-model, and so the A-6 designation became assigned to a new fighter version. The origins of this variant lay in a call for a 'heavy' fighter for use on the Eastern Front, but this plan was adapted or switched for use in the West and over the Reich, where it was felt such a configuration could be deployed against the increasing numbers of American daylight bombers. It would be used in this role initially by the specialist bomber attack unit *Sturmstaffel* 1.

Powered by a 1700hp BMW 801D-2 engine, the Fw 190A-6 entered production in the summer of 1943 and was built under licence by AGO at Oschersleben, Arado at Warnemünde and Fieseler at Kassel.

The standard fuel load – and thus range – was enhanced by the installation of a centreline ETC 501 bomb rack under the fuselage between the wheel bays, to which could be hung a 300-litre drop tank manufactured by FRB Erla in Antwerp that added another 240kg of weight when laden with fuel.

Standard armament consisted of two fuselage-mounted Rheinmetall-Borsig 7.92mm MG 17 machine guns, for which tracer ammunition allowed Luftwaffe pilots to sharpen their aim while using wing cannon. Indeed, one of the main design advantages of the A-6 was to be the modified, lighter wing which featured a flattened bulge into which could be installed a total of four fast-firing 20mm Mauser MG 151/20 cannon – one in each wing root and one in each of the outer sections, each with 140 rounds per gun. The MG 151/20s were intended to replace the old, slower-firing Ikaria MG FF cannon (the rate of fire of the latter being 530 rounds per minute, and the former 680–750 rounds per minute). Ejection chutes were fitted, as was an EK 16 Robot camera in the wing leading edge.

Designed by Otto Helmuth von Lossnitzer and Dr Doerge, joint directors of Waffenfabrik Mauser A.G., the electrically cocked and fired MG 151 was

A fine Focke-Wulf works photograph showing a BMW 801 radial engine unit complete with cowling ring – a so-called 'power egg' – suspended from a hoist and chains, about to be installed onto an Fw 190 airframe which is jacked up with its mainwheels just clear of the floor. Another engine unit is visible on a trolley just behind, ready for assembly. Note the port side 7.92mm MG 17 machine gun. Fabric padding has been wedged between the raised gun access panel and the front windscreen for protection. (EN Archive)

capable of discharging 86kg of ammunition in flight at a muzzle velocity of 900m per second. The weapon was recoil-operated and belt-fed, using a disintegrating metallic link belt. The MG 151 weighed 42.4kg.

Two fuselage-mounted 7.9mm machine guns were also retained, and the aircraft featured additional protective armour around the cockpit. It could be equipped with FuG 16ZE (as standard) and FuG 25 radio equipment.

Two fighter sub-types were produced. The A-6/R1 was fitted with a WB 151/20 gondola under each wing, carrying two MG 151s with 130 rounds per gun per gondola. With such heavy armament, the aircraft was intended as a *Pulkzerstörer* (formation destroyer). Overall weight increased from 3930kg to 4310kg. The conversion was carried out at the *Luftzeugamt* (aircraft department), a subsidiary of Arado, at Küpper, near Sagan in Silesia.

An Fw 190 under assembly. View of the mainwheel housing on the underside of the port wing and the associated hydraulics, with the wheel covering door lowered. Also seen here is the barrel of the 20mm MG 151/20 wing root cannon protruding from the wing leading edge. Each of the two such weapons installed were armed with 250 rounds. (EN Archive)

An Fw 190A-6, still carrying its callsign code KS+ME, being serviced and rearmed by groundcrew. The access panels for the MG 151/20 outer wing cannon are lowered and armourers in the foreground have pulled out a belt of shells from an ammunition box. The starboard side panel allowing access to the BMW 801 engine is also open and an external fuel tank lies on the grass beneath the port wing. (EN Archive)

Around 60 machines had been converted by 31 November 1943, with the first going to 3./JG 11.

Leutnant Richard Franz who flew with *Sturmstaffel* 1 and JG 11 felt that:

The later variants of the Fw 190A proved to be very good aircraft in the '*Sturm*' role due to their armament and additional armour plating. The radial engine also gave some protection. Due to its heaviness, however, the Focke-Wulf showed a

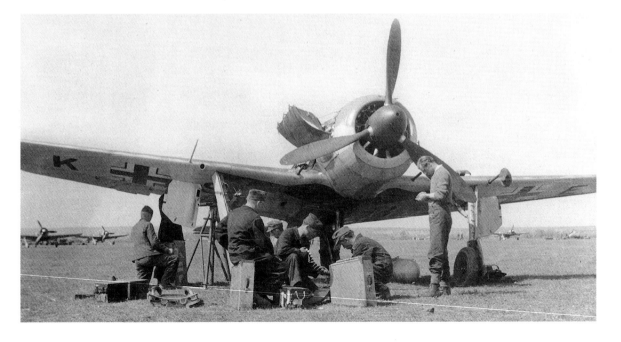

Fw 190A-8/R2 WING GUNS

The Fw 190A-7, A-8 and A-9 variants fielded a pair of fuselage-mounted Rheinmetall-Borsig 13mm MG 131 machine guns, supplemented with four Mauser 20mm MG 151/20E cannon in the wing roots and outer wing. The A-8/R2, depicted here, saw the MG 151s replaced by 30mm MK 108s that were better suited to close-range operations against four-engined bombers, while the A-8/R3 carried a Rheinmetall 30mm MK 103 cannon in a pod under each wing that had a rate of fire of 450 rounds per minute.

great disadvantage when engaging enemy fighters. In the normal configuration, the Fw 190 had some advantage in comparison with the Bf 109 up to 4570m, whereas the Bf 109 was better at higher altitudes.

The A-6/R2 carried a Rheinmetall-Borsig MK 108 30mm *Maschinenkanone* – a blow-back operated, rear-seared, belt-fed cannon, using electric ignition, being charged and triggered by compressed air – in each wing. The prime benefit of this weapon, used profusely by the Luftwaffe for close-range anti-

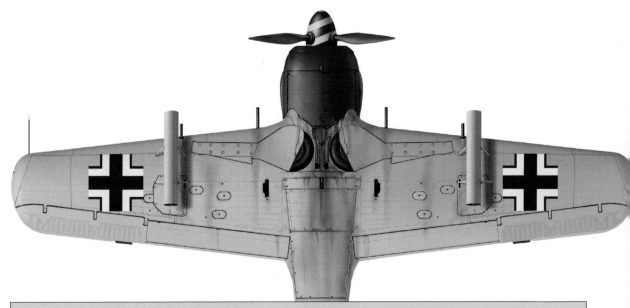

Fw 190A-7/8/9 W.Gr.21 UNDERWING MORTARS

Many Fw 190s were fitted with tubes to fire W.Gr.21 mortars. These were adapted infantry weapons intended to break up a bomber formation by blast effect, thus diminishing enemy defensive fire. One 1.3m-long rifled mortar launching tube was suspended from beneath each underside wing surface of an Fw 190 by means of four bracing lugs and a central hook with a suspension bracket. Three retaining springs, located near the rear end of the tube, held the 112kg shell, with its 40kg

warhead, in place. A screw bolt, also at the rear end of the tube, prevented the shell from sliding out. In an emergency, the launching tube could be jettisoned by activating an electrically primed explosive charge which severed the central hook.

The mortars were controlled from a cockpit armament panel containing two armament switches and a Revi 16B reflector sight. Two spin-stabilised shells were fired simultaneously when the pilot depressed a button on his control column.

bomber work over northwest and southern Europe from early 1942 onwards, lay in its simplicity and economic process of manufacture, the greater part of its components consisting of pressed sheet metal stampings. At only half the weight of the larger and longer 30mm MK 103 wing-mounted cannon, two MK 108s represented the same payload but had a combined rate of fire slightly more than three times that of a single MK 103.

The MK 108 quickly earned a fearsome reputation amongst both German pilots and Allied bomber crews, the latter dubbing it the 'pneumatic hammer'. However, just one A-6/R2 was completed, the Fw 190 V51, which also became the prototype for the ensuing Fw 190A-7/R2.

The A-6/R3 was fitted for trials only with a single MK 103 beneath each wing carrying 25 rounds per gun. Another sub-type, commencing from November 1943, was the A-6/R6, which used a retro-conversion pack for the fitment of underwing 21cm *Werfer-Granate* (W.Gr.) 21 air-to-air mortars that became standard on the A-6 from February 1944.

For its role as a close-range bomber-destroyer, the A-6 was also fitted with additional 50mm armoured plates on either side of the cockpit, and 30mm

Fw 190A-7 Wk-Nr 642545 VQ+VC was the 200th such aircraft to be finished by the Gerhard Fieseler company at Kassel (note the '200' applied to the fuselage *Balkenkreuz*) and formed part of that factory's first production batch built in November–December 1943. Along with Fieseler, the A-7 was manufactured by Focke-Wulf at Sorau, Marienburg and Cottbus and AGO at Oschersleben. (EN Archive)

Panzerglas (armoured glass) panels were fitted to each side of the cockpit canopy. These fitments seem to have been carried out at unit level, for in photographs the armoured side panels do not appear to be of uniform size.

Another sub-variant – the A-6/R4 – featured a GM1 nitrous oxide injection power boost system for the BMW 801 engine.

Production of the A-6 continued until late November/early December 1943, when it was superseded by the Fw 190A-7. Around 1192 machines were built.

In the following short-run, interim A-7 variant, which commenced production at Fieseler and Ago in November 1943, the main change was the replacement of the cowl-mounted MG 17s with a pair of 13mm MG 131s with 475 rounds per gun. These necessitated the incorporation of extended longitudinal bulges with access panels to house the new, larger weapons. In the A-7, the R1 is believed to have never been built, while the R2 carried two MK 108 wing guns with 55 rounds per gun. It is thought that the R2 conversion accounted for half the production run of just 80 or so aircraft built by Focke-Wulf at Cottbus, Ago and Fieseler. The aircraft was intended for deployment against Allied heavy bombers, with examples being delivered to JG 1, JG 2, JG 11 and JG 26 from early March 1944. Ten such variants were completed by Fieseler in November 1943, with 20 in December and 30 in January 1944. It is unlikely that the MK 103-equipped R3 was delivered for use. The A-7/R6 replicated the A-6/R6 with half of the production run being fitted for mortar configuration.

Externally, an ETC 501 centreline rack was fitted for the carrying of a 300-litre drop tank to extend range, and provisions were made on some examples for a completely revised tailwheel arrangement. In the cockpit, the Revi C/12D gunsight was replaced by the new Reflexvisier Revi 16B sight. To use this device, the pilot

The forward construction of the 14-cylinder, air-cooled BMW 801 radial engine is clearly visible in this photograph of an Fw 190 of II./JG 1 undergoing maintenance in a hangar at an operational airfield. The propeller hub has been removed. (EN Archive)

This Fw 190A-8 of an unidentified fighter unit has its upper and lower engine access panels open while undergoing servicing at a Luftwaffe airfield. Visible on the other side of the aircraft are the wheels of a generator cart which has been plugged into the fuselage connection socket. Note that the barrels of the wing guns have been capped. (EN Archive)

viewed a target through an optical collimator projecting onto a tilted panel of flat glass. This formed an aiming point at an infinite optical distance, allowing the image to be independent of the pilot's head position. The Revi 16B had larger lenses and a more powerful bulb that gave improved definition. A simplified radio system with no screening was fitted.

By far the most numerous and most potent Fw 190 fighter to be built (1334 aircraft produced between Focke-Wulf at Cottbus and Aslau, Ago, Fieseler, Weserflug at Tempelhof and Norddeutsche Dornier at Wismar), the A-8, which also had the most sub-variants, was the Luftwaffe's main close-range interceptor, or *Sturmflugzeug* (assault aircraft) or *Sturmjäger* (assault fighter), for operations against heavy bombers throughout 1944–45. In its handbook on the aircraft, the Luftwaffe describes the A-8 thus:

> The Fw 190A-8 is a single-seat fighter aircraft possessing both a high top speed and good manoeuvrability. It can also be deployed as a fighter-bomber carrying bombs, or as an extended-range fighter carrying an under-fuselage drop tank. It is a single-engined, cantilever low-wing monoplane, of all-metal construction, with a single vertical tail and retractable undercarriage.

Powered by a 1700hp BMW 801D-2 14-cylinder, two-row, radial air-cooled engine with two-stage supercharger, reduction gearing and cooling fan, it could attain a maximum speed of 647km/h at 5500m, reaching 656km/h with GM 1 nitrous oxygen boost. A control unit – the *Kommandogerät* ('command device') – automatically adjusted and monitored propeller RPM, boost pressure, fuel mixture, ignition timing adjustment and supercharger switchover. The three-bladed adjustable propeller, 3.30m in diameter, was provided with a constant speed unit. If the automatic adjustment controls or engine failed, the blades could be electrically positioned by a thumb-actuated manual switch.

Fuel was held in two self-sealing tanks beneath the cockpit of 232 and 292 litres, respectively, but another 115 litres could be carried in the area normally assigned to the GM 1 fuel tank or the MW 50 methanol-water power-boosting system. Range was 1035km at 7000m, extending to 1470km when carrying a 300-litre drop tank.

Feldwebel Oscar Bösch, who would fly the Fw 190 with *Sturmstaffel* 1 and IV./JG 3, recalled:

> The Fw 190 was an excellent fighter. It was most reliable and very robust. It was also beautiful to fly. From my own personal encounters with the enemy, I was never out-manoeuvred. It was, of course, difficult to compare with other aircraft in action as a) we were out-numbered by far, b) we were usually out-positioned and c) over-worked and over-stressed. But in general the P-51 Mustang was our most feared and dangerous opponent in every respect – at high and low altitudes. We found that the Mustang was faster than our Fw 190A-8s, so our aircraft were fitted with a power boost methanol-water injection system, which was relatively efficient, giving us ten per cent more power, but only for five minutes. Then the MK 108 guns were gradually changed for MG 151/20s, which were much lighter than the MK 108s which would often jam during a high-G turn. Our armourers found that the weight of the rounds in the MK 108 would tear the ammunition feed.

The A-8 handbook continued:

> The fuselage is composed of a Dural covering over a monocoque frame. At its forward end it is of circular cross-section to match the shape of the powerplant. At the rear end it is of oval cross-section. It comprises two major sub-sections, the forward fuselage (firewall to bulkhead 8) and the rear fuselage (bulkhead 8 to bulkhead 14). The engine bearer assembly is attached to the firewall (bulkhead 1). The cockpit and fuel tanks are housed in the forward fuselage. In an emergency, the cockpit canopy can be jettisoned by the actuation of an explosive charge. Armour plating protects the pilot against enemy fire. An equipment bay, accessible through a hinged cover, is located in the rear fuselage. A fabric bulkhead, also located in the aft fuselage, prevents the sucking of engine exhaust fumes forward into the cockpit.

Armament was formidable. Although the standard configuration was based on the A-7 with two 13mm MG 131 machine guns in the upper cowling with 475 rounds per gun, the A-8 could be converted to an R1 with four wing-mounted MG 151s – two in the wing roots carrying 250 rounds per gun and two such weapons in the outer sections with 140 rounds per gun. However, due to an ensuing reduction in performance, series production of the R1 was discontinued on 8 April 1944. The A-8/R2 saw the MG 151s replaced by 30mm MK 108s in underwing pods, as the latter were better suited to close-

The bulkiness of the side armoured glass panel framework as fitted to the canopy of the Fw 190A-8/R8 is clearly visible here. Also seen is the pilot's rear seat armour. (EN Archive)

range destructive work. The A-8/R3 carried a single gas-operated, air-cooled Rheinmetall 30mm MK 103 cannon in a pod under each wing, having a rate of fire of 450 rounds per minute. Like the MK 108, the MK 103 had parts stamped out of sheet metal.

The A-8/R7 carried five-millimetre armour plating around the MK 108s and cockpit, as well as 30mm *Panzerglas* (armoured glass) side panels in the canopy. The A-8/R8 was a *Sturmflugzeug* – 'assault aircraft' – which included armoured glass and a built-in MK 108 in the wing outboard position. Commonplace also on the A-8 were twin underwing 21cm mortars, the fittings for which were built in as standard.

Radio equipment comprised the FuG 16 ZY VHF transceiver with a Morane whip aerial array and, from June 1944, a 16mm BSK (*Ballistische Schußmeßkammer*) 16 camera was installed in the leading edge of the port wing between the cannon.

Willi Unger took a pragmatic view of the introduction of the Fw 190 into service with IV./JG 3:

I flew about half of my operations with the Bf 109G-6, which could operate from any airfield in Germany. It could also be flown successfully in *Gruppe* formation against the *Viermots*. But the disadvantages of the Bf 109 were its narrow undercarriage and its vulnerability to hits in its radiator system. Its main advantage over the Fw 190 was its superiority at high altitudes.

From mid-May 1944, IV. *Gruppe* was re-equipped with the Fw 190A-8. From then onwards IV. *Gruppe* was known as the IV.(*Sturm*)/JG 3 *Udet*. This was the first *Sturmgruppe* to be put into operations against the *Viermots*. The A-8 was designed intentionally as a heavy fighter with a mix of machine guns and cannon. It was also strengthened with steel armour plating around the cockpit and with armoured glass panels. This made the Fw 190 a robust, heavy fighter, and fully capable of operations against *Viermots* from most types of airfield.

Advantages – wide undercarriage, large, twin-row radial engine which protected the pilot from fire from the front, an electric starter motor and electric trim system. Disadvantages – there was a danger of turning over when braking hard on soft or sandy ground. In combat against enemy fighters it was more cumbersome because of the armour plating. It was manoeuvrable at low altitude, but inferior to the Bf 109 at higher altitudes.

The Fw 190A-8 was flown operationally by *Stab*, I. and II./JG 1, *Stab*, I. and III./JG 2, *Stab* and IV./JG 3, *Stab* and II./JG 4, *Stab*, I. and II./JG 6, *Stab*, I., III. and 10./JG 11, *Stab*, I. and II./JG 26, *Stab* and II./JG 300, *Stab*, I., II. and III./JG 301, I./JG 302, *Sturmstaffel* 1, *Erprobungskommando* 25 and *Jagdgruppe* 10.

CHAPTER 5
ART OF WAR

In November 1942, the Fw 190 provided a timely and effective gun platform for the Luftwaffe as VIII Bomber Command gradually escalated its 'heavy' bombing operations over western Europe. As such, the Luftwaffe was forced to devise reactive tactics to counter the threat, and one engagement between Fw 190s and B-17s served to mould German tactical doctrine.

On 23 November, a force of 36 unescorted heavy bombers set out to bomb the Saint-Nazaire U-boat pens. During the course of the mission they were attacked by Fw 190s from Hauptmann Egon Mayer's III./JG 2, which had intentionally assembled into formations of three aircraft known as *Ketten*. It was the *Gruppenkommandeur* himself who led his unit towards the bombers, approaching from head-on and a little to the left. When his Fw 190A-4 was in range, Mayer opened fire with a no-deflection burst that gave him the impression that his cone of fire was reaching the area in front of the enemy aircraft. In pulling up to the left, he observed hits in the starboard wing area of the B-17. The wing broke away and the Flying Fortress turned over and spun in, exploding as it went down.

Crucially, Mayer had experienced no defensive fire as he made his approach. Following their attack, the German pilots then made sharp pulls up to the left or right, and again, at first, there was no defensive fire, but this was followed by heavy fire as the Focke-Wulfs moved over or beneath and behind the bombers using a climb or half-roll. After this initial attack, several more passes were flown against other B-17s in the formation from the front. In a final attack, strikes were seen in the fuselage areas and wing roots. In turning under one Flying Fortress, Mayer saw a 'light ball of fire' beneath the aircraft, moments after which the bomber 'spun in, twisting and turning and exploding after receiving more hits from the rear.'

Next, Mayer aimed for the small formation of B-24s which were also flying that day, attacking one from ahead and to one side, keeping his speed as low as possible. As he opened fire on the Liberator, Mayer skidded his Fw 190 in the direction of flight of the B-24 by applying simple rudder movement. Violent

Amidst a field of wheat in northern France, the *Kommodore* of JG 2, Major Egon Mayer, stands on the starboard wing of B-17F 42-3190 of the 332nd BS/ 94th BG that he shot down on 13 July 1943 – one of two the ace claimed that day. In late 1942, it was Mayer, at the time *Kommandeur* of III./JG 2, who convinced Generalmajor Adolf Galland that a frontal pass against a B-17 offered the best chance of bringing it down. The relatively intact Flying Fortress seen here would have been examined and stripped of parts of tactical or technical interest and use. (EN Archive)

explosions were seen from the first shots, and the American bomber 'pulled up slightly and dived straight down without spinning. No one bailed out.'

Mayer believed that a frontal pass, as opposed to the customary rearward attack, offered the best chance to inflict damage on the bombers' vulnerable cockpit area. Even more importantly, the frontal arc of defensive fire was the weakest. Four bombers went down following the attack for the loss of only one Fw 190.

Encouraged by this initial success, from this point on Galland believed that the usual method of attacking from the rear promised scant success and invariably resulted in losses. He felt that in cases where German pilots were compelled to carry out such an attack, it should be made from above or below, and the fuel tanks and engines should be the aiming points. Comparatively, an attack directed at the side of a bomber could be effective, but required thorough training and good gunnery. Galland was so convinced by what Mayer and his pilots had demonstrated that he issued a notice to all fighter units informing them that an attack from the front, mounted front high or front low, conducted at low speed was the most effective. He added that 'flying ability, good aiming and closing up to the shortest possible range are the prerequisites for success.'

Importantly, he also stated (author's italics):

> Basically, the strongest weapon is the *massed and repeated attack by an entire fighter formation*. In such cases, the defensive fire can be weakened and the bomber formation broken up.

This would become Galland's firm mantra over the coming months. However, in reality, at this time encounters between Luftwaffe fighters and American bomber formations were either fast, short, sporadic affairs – especially if, as had started happening from May 1943, fighter escort was present – or massed but swirling, wild melees in which discipline in formation and coordination broke down and attacks became frantic and mounted from all angles.

German tactics seemed to sway between attacks from the rear and from head-on. Those pilots electing to mount rearward attacks found that the most vulnerable spot on a four-engined bomber was the wing area between the fuselage and the inboard engines. The No. 3 engine on a B-17 was considered particularly important because it powered the hydraulic system.

In executing the head-on attack, which many units preferred, the cockpit and – once again – the No. 3 engine became the most important targets. However, in August 1943, the *Oberkomnmando der Luftwaffe* (OKL – Luftwaffe High Command) reversed Galland's instructions and ordered that all attacks mounted against heavy bombers must be made from the rear, rather than by a frontal pass. This was chiefly because, in the OKL's view, many of the young, inexperienced pilots now equipping the *Jagdgeschwader* operating in the defence of the Reich and over the West found it difficult to undertake the latter type of attack. The frontal pass involved a high combined closing speed which, in turn, demanded great skill in gunnery, range estimation and flying control.

Yet by October 1943 I. *Jagdkorps* recorded that, 'the numerically inferior German daytime fighter units failed to prevent a single American large-scale raid during October 1943.' This worrying state of affairs had not failed to escape the attention of Major Hans-Günter von Kornatzki, an officer on Galland's staff.

Von Kornatzki had studied reels of gun camera film, read combat reports describing attacks on *Viermots* and interviewed pilots. He reasoned that during a rearward attack against an American heavy bomber formation, one German fighter was potentially exposed to the defensive fire of more than 40 American 0.50-cal. machine guns, resulting in only the slimmest chance of escaping damage. Under such circumstances, it was even less likely that a lone fighter could bring down a bomber. However, if a complete *Gruppe* could position itself for an attack at close range, the bomber gunners would be forced to disperse their fire, and thus weaken it, allowing individual fighters greater opportunity to close in, avoid damage and shoot a bomber down. The loss of speed and manoeuvrability incurred by the extra armament and armour carried by these *Sturm* aircraft would be countered by the presence of two regular fighter *Gruppen* that would keep any escorts at bay.

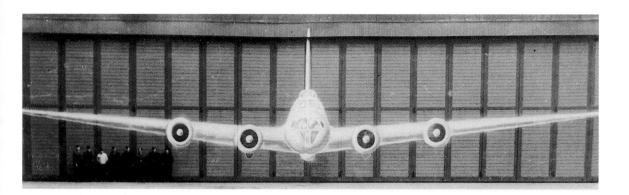

A scale mural of a B-17 painted across the sectionalised doors of a hangar at a Luftwaffe fighter base. This would have been used for gunnery training and range familiarisation purposes. From mid-1943 the priority for German fighter units operating over northwest Europe became the destruction of the Allied *Viermots*. Note the eight groundcrewmen lined up just beneath the starboard wing of the bomber. (EN Archive)

Von Kornatzki also suggested to Galland that if necessary, and as a last-ditch resort in instances where pilots were close enough and if ammunition had been expended, a bomber could be rammed in order to bring it down. He further proposed that a smaller unit, a *Staffel*, first be established to train up volunteer pilots who would test and evaluate the new method using Fw 190s under operational conditions. It seems Galland needed little convincing. He immediately authorised the establishment of the first *Sturmstaffel*, to be known as *Sturmstaffel* 1, and appointed von Kornatzki its commander. On 8 November 1943, he signalled his fighter leaders that the objective of the new *Staffel* was:

> . . . to break up Allied formations by means of an all-out attack with more heavily-armed fighters in close formation and at the closest range. Such attacks that are undertaken are to be pressed home to the very heart of the Allied formation whatever happens and without regard to losses until the formation is annihilated.

By November 1943, the first cadre of pilots was arriving at the *Staffel*'s base at Achmer, where they were required to sign an oath ensuring that they would carry out their combat missions at the closest range in formation. If they were unsuccessful in their attack they were to ram a bomber as 'the only alternative'. The *Sturm* pilot was to remain with the damaged bomber until they collided.

Leutnant Richard Franz recalled how difficult it was to shoot down a heavy bomber in conditions such as those prevailing in late 1943–early 1944:

> At this time, the *Sturmstaffel* was the only unit in the Luftwaffe which attacked bombers from the rear flying in a 'V' formation. The close 'V' formation provided a very strong attacking force with extreme firepower, so that when we engaged we were always successful. On one hand, unlike the usual head-on tactic, this gave us much more time to attack and shoot, but on the other hand, the Fortress gunners had the same advantage. In my opinion – and as I recall – the defensive bomber formation was very effective, because in trying to attack it, it was very difficult to find even one angle at which you were not subject to defensive fire. In addition, flying at the outer perimeters of the formation, there was often what we called a 'Flak cruiser' – an aircraft without bombs but carrying additional machine guns and cannon.

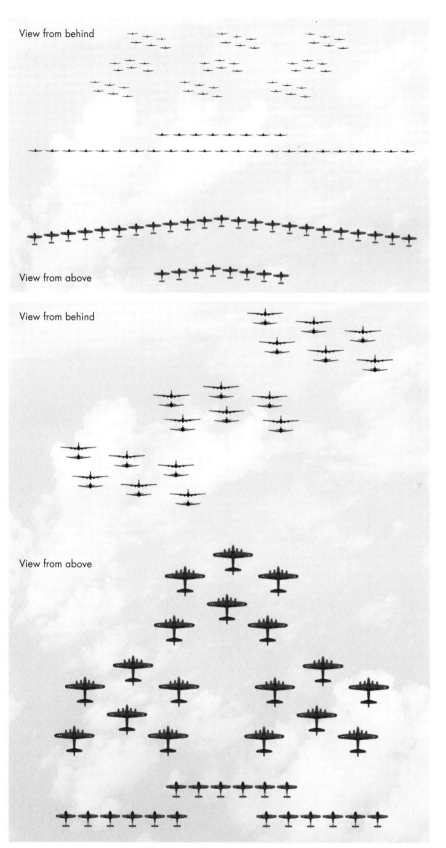

View from behind

View from above

View from behind

View from above

This view, from behind and above, shows a typical anti-heavy bomber formation attack by a *Sturmgruppe*. The latter, comprising a *Stab* and three *Staffeln*, makes a massed, line abreast (or in USAAF terms, a 'Company Front') approach towards the bomber formation from behind. The escort to the Fw 190s, either more Fw 190s (as depicted here) or Bf 109s, flies above and behind the *Sturmgruppe*.

The attack formation breaks into three sections as it closes in with the bombers, with each Fw 190 *Sturmgruppe* pilot targeting a bomber in the low, lead and high flights. The Fw 190s make their attack and pass through the formation. They will then try and re-form for a second attacking pass.

Another problem was trying to bring our very heavy birds into position before we were caught by the escort fighters, which sometimes happened, causing us severe losses. It was the P-51s and P-47s that caused us the heaviest losses in our *Staffel*. Their control was very good, the tactical direction of their leaders was good and their endurance was much higher than ours in most cases.

These tactics were justified as long as the *Sturm* fighters could *get close enough* to the bombers without the risk of being intercepted by escort fighters on their approach, or being deflected or damaged by mass defensive fire from the bombers. Furthermore, by the spring of 1944 the main problem facing the Luftwaffe's home defence fighter units was the sheer mass of aircraft – bombers and escorts – which the Eighth Air Force was able to field. The task of shooting bombers down became increasingly difficult.

Thus, the principle of the '*Gefechtsverband*' (battle formation), a large composite formation of fighters, was tabled as a means with which to tackle mass with mass. In this regard, the *Gruppen* of JG 3 often flew into action alongside the heavily armed and armoured Fw 190A-6s and A-7s of *Sturmstaffel* 1.

Typically, if, in the opinion of the German fighter controllers, prevailing clear weather allowed the possibility of an incoming daylight raid, and if German radar and listening services had detected enemy formations or radio traffic, the *Gefechtsverbandführer* or the *Kommodore* of a *Jagdgeschwader* which operated a *Sturmgruppe* would be telephoned and instructed to place his entire formation on 15 minutes readiness. The formation leader would then relay this information to his *Gruppenkommandeure*, who, in turn, would hold a pre-briefing with their pilots.

Once confirmation of an incoming raid had been received from the *Jagddivision* – usually at the point when enemy bombers were either assembling or crossing the English coast – the *Geschwader* would go onto three minutes readiness. As more information arrived, the pilots would move forward to *Sitzbereitschaft,* or cockpit readiness, and be appraised of further developments via loudspeaker at the dispersal point.

At the order to scramble, all three *Gruppen* would then take off and assemble over their own airfields at an altitude of 900–1800m within six to ten minutes, before flying to the *Gefechtsverband* assembly point, where, under strict radio discipline and control, the *Gefechtsverbandführer* formed up the whole battle formation. The formation assembly usually took place at 3000m, and had to be complete within about 20 minutes. The formation would then climb to a combat altitude of 7500–8000m. In the case of IV.(*Sturm*)/JG 3, following assembly, the *Gruppe*'s Fw 190s flew in two stacked-down Vee or *Sturmkeil* (storm wedge) formations each comprising of eight to ten aircraft (depending on serviceability), the second formation flying 140–180m behind and about 45m below the lead formation.

Meanwhile, the Bf 109 *Begleitgruppen* (escorts) would split to either side of the *Sturmgruppe*, stacked up from front to rear. Another, smaller escort would fly high cover at about 900m above the rearmost aircraft of the second Vee of the *Sturmgruppe*. The Bf 109s would fly in a sufficiently loose formation to avoid slipstreams and allow aircraft to weave without the risk of collision.

Within sight of the enemy bomber formation and some 90–150m above and 900–1520m behind it, the *Sturmgruppe* would drop its external tanks, then re-form from its Vee formation into its line abreast *Angriffsformation* (attack formation) or *Breitkeil* (wide wedge). This was carried out by climbing where necessary and fanning out into a slightly swept-back line abreast formation of usually more than 20 fighters, either level with or slightly above the enemy, with the commander of the *Gruppe* and his deputy flying at its apex.

However, throughout May 1944, I. *Jagdkorps* still found it increasingly difficult to concentrate its forces against large American raids as its units were scattered across the Reich, had to fly great distances to reach the bombers and required long periods to assemble into *Gefechtsvervbände*. Consequently, German fighters were often late in intercepting the *Viermots*, or were forced to land early as a result of fuel shortage. Feldwebel Willi Unger of 11./JG 3 recalled:

Three flights of B-17s are silhouetted against the sky as a lone P-51 Mustang escort fighter flies close to its charges. Once the Mustang appeared over Europe at the end of 1943, the stakes raised significantly and gravely for the fighter units of the *Reichsverteidigung*. (Author's Collection)

The operational bases of our fighter units in the *Reichsverteidigung* were spread all over Germany. Attempts to maintain strength at critical times and in critical areas were made by the rapid redeployment of fighters to northern or southern Germany. Several *Gruppen* would combine together in the air from various airfields and were then led together from the ground to attack the approaching bombers. This did not always work. The bombers often 'cheated' by flying towards one town, then changing their course and bombing a completely different target. As the flying endurance of our fighters with an auxiliary drop tank was a maximum of 2.5 hours, we were often forced to break off. There is no question of German fighters having the advantage – only disadvantages, since the numbers of American escort fighters were far superior to us, and they also operated at higher altitude, to our disadvantage.

Major Anton Hackl, the *Gruppenkommandeur* of the Fw 190-equipped III./JG 11, a recipient of the Oak Leaves to the Knight's Cross with more than 150 victories to his credit, was one of the Luftwaffe's principal tacticians and a leading 'bomber killer'. On 20 May 1944, he sent a paper to Galland in which he offered his suggestions on what tactics he felt were required to combat the *Viermots*. He believed that systematic, repeated attacks should be made against

A *Rotte*, or pair, of Fw 190s head out on another long-range sortie carrying drop tanks. The *Rotte* formed the smallest tactical flight element comprising the leader and his wingman. Two *Rotten* would form a *Schwarm*. Often, much fuel would be consumed as large fighter formations raced across distances to join up with other units or tried to locate incoming enemy bombers. (EN Archive)

a bomber formation to weaken its escort and defence, but also to allow the surviving stream to fly deeper into Reich airspace so that:

. . . rear attacks are then possible, so that even bad gunners would have to get a victory or be suspected of cowardice. Experience of frontal attacks show that only older (experienced) pilots get victories and, for the most part, they get hit. Younger pilots do not approach correctly, nor go in near enough.

Feldwebel Oscar Bösch commenced combat operations flying with *Sturmstaffel* 1 at the end of April, before being reassigned as part of IV./JG 3. He recounted:

In the beginning, attacking the bombers was almost easy. It was exciting. Your adrenalin really pumped. Everybody had their own tactics, their own tricks, but generally we attacked from behind and high for additional speed, offset by five to ten degrees and about 500m above the formation, opening fire upon the order by radio at 400m. The air was pretty thin at 7200m, and often there was a lot of turbulence behind the bomber formation. This sometimes made our approach very difficult. Positioning was also made difficult because of the escort fighters. [Oberleutnant Othmar] Zehart, for example, had guts. He flew right into the *Pulk* and we just followed him in.

When the escort fighters were late to react, we had time to line up – like being on parade – before diving to attack. The bomber gunners usually started to fire and waste their ammunition while we were still out of range at 2000m from them. It was obvious they were just as scared as we were. Shaken by the slipstream of the B-17s and blinded by condensation trails, we were subjected to machine gun fire for minutes or seconds that seemed endless before being able to see the results of our attack. Despite the armour plating of our cockpits, we had good reason to dread the defensive fire of the bombers.

We always went in line abreast. That was our normal tactic. If you went in singly, all the bombers shot at you with their massive defensive firepower, and you drew fire from the waist gunners. But as an attack formation, the psychological effect on the bomber gunners was much greater.

First of all, you tried to knock out the tail gunner. Then you went for the intersection between wing and fuselage, and you just kept at it, watching your hits flare and flare again. It all happened so quickly. You gave it all you had. Sometimes, after the first attack, all your energy seemed to go. Your nerves were burned out. But we had this kind of theory that when you were in the middle of a bomber formation – flying through it – you were, in a way, 'protected'. The bombers wouldn't open fire because they didn't want to shoot at their own aircraft.

We would break off the attack just before we were about to collide with our target. The devastating effect of our 30mm guns was such that we would often fly through a rain of fragments, some being complete sections of aircraft.

CHAPTER 6
COMBAT

On the first day of January 1944, *Sturmstaffel* 1 was at Dortmund, having relocated there from Achmer, where it reported 14 Fw 190A-6s on strength, of which 11 were serviceable. In terms of its aircraft type, the *Staffel* joined *Stab*, I. and II./JG 1, III./JG 11, *Stab* and II./JG 300 and II./JG 302 – all deployed under the newly formed *Luftflotte Reich*, which had responsibility for the coordination and control of the fighter units operating in defence of the central homeland. Most of these units also had a number of A-7s and, collectively, they fielded around 141 Fw 190s. They would bear the brunt of fighting the USAAF's bomber formations over Reich territory.

The first encounter of the year with the American bombers took place on 4 January when VIII Bomber Command sent 313 B-17s and 132 B-24s, carrying 1000 tons of bombs, to attack the port area at Kiel, although according to the USAAF:

A Luftwaffe NCO directs groundcrew as they push an Fw 190A-7 of I./JG 1 back towards its dispersal at Dortmund in January 1944. The aircraft's nose is adorned with the distinctive black and white horizontal bars of the *Geschwader* and carries that unit's winged '1' emblem on its nose. (EN Archive)

The primary effort on this day was against Kiel, with a two Combat Wing force breaking from the lead position over the North Sea to attack Münster from the northeast. The misleading direction of this secondary thrust, together with adverse weather conditions, appears to have hindered the enemy substantially in effecting a concentration against the Kiel force.

However, given their location at Rheine, only 50km to the north of Münster, it is highly likely that the Fw 190s of II./JG 1 would have been directed by 3. *Jagddivision* towards the Münster force. At 1005 hrs, the *Gruppe* was given the *Alarmstart* and made course towards the city. Fifteen minutes later, two *Pulks* of around 40 B-17s – probably the two detached Combat Wings – with strong fighter escort were sighted southwest of Münster at 7000m heading west, presumably having completed their mission. Leading a *Rotte* of Fw 190s from 4./JG 1 at 4000m was Feldwebel Heinz Fuchs:

> As we approached the Boeings, I pulled up from below towards a B-17 that was about 500m to the rear of the formation. Although the Thunderbolt fighter cover was flying only some 100m above, I was able to make two attacks from behind and into a very close range. The right outboard engine [of the B-17] stopped and parts of the fuselage and empennage flew away. The Boeing then lost a lot of altitude.
>
> During a third attack from the side, I was attacked by Thunderbolts. A third of my right aileron was shot off and my aircraft also received several hits in the wing and tail unit, so that I was forced to land. The B-17 that I attacked was last seen by my wingman, Oberfeldwebel Liper, flying at an altitude of 2000m. Its crash took place at 1200 hrs.

Fuchs was credited with his eighth aerial victory, but it was the only one awarded to JG 1 that day. I. *Jagdkorps* had mounted 327 sorties and lost 12 aircraft, with seven pilots killed. The USAAF lost 17 bombers.

On the morning of the 5th, the German early warning system reported large American formations assembling over England. Just like the day before, which marked the first daylight raid against a German target in the New Year, Kiel was to be attacked. Escorted by 70 P-38 Lightnings, 119 B-17s of the 1st BD and 96 B-24s of the 2nd BD set out to bomb the city's shipyards. The visual attack enabled a good concentration of bombs to hit their assigned target.

But the flight to Kiel was not without adversity. At 1000 hrs, the first German fighters were scrambled to intercept. The *Geschwaderkommodore*, high-scoring ace Oberstleutnant Walter Oesau, immediately made his presence felt by sharing in the destruction of a B-24 with his wingman, but I./JG 1 was kept on the ground for two hours. When the *Gruppe* did finally take off, it met the first elements of the bomber formation over Belgium at 1245 hrs and subsequently scored one victory and four B-17 *Herausschusse*. However, I./JG 1 paid a heavy price, having three of its pilots killed. The day also proved to be an inauspicious debut for *Sturmstaffel* 1, which made no contact with the enemy and returned to Dortmund.

On 11 January a force of 663 USAAF bombers flew in deteriorating conditions to strike at aviation and industrial targets in the heart of the Reich at Oschersleben, Halberstadt, Braunschweig and Osnabrück. This mission marked the commencement of Operation *Pointblank*, the strategic air offensive against Germany designed to bring about 'the progressive destruction and dislocation of the German military and economic system.'

Alerted about the impending raid, *Sturmstaffel* 1 and I./JG 1 transferred from Dortmund to Rheine and waited for the order to take off. It came at 1030 hrs. Thirty minutes later I./JG 1 executed a frontal attack

The emblem of *Sturmstaffel* 1 – a shield on which is portrayed a mailed gauntlet clutching a lightning bolt over a cloud set against a blue background – has been applied to this Fw 190. (EN Archive)

against the bombers and shot down three in as many minutes between 1108 and 1110 hrs. The *Sturmstaffel* separated from I./JG 1 and, in conformity with its intended tactical doctrine, attacked an American combat box from the rear. Approaching at close range, Oberleutnant Othmar Zehart opened fire simultaneously with the other pilots of the *Staffel* and shot down a B-17, the first victory for his unit.

After being at cockpit readiness for some time, 15 Fw 190s of II./JG 1 took off at 1030 hrs led by 23-year-old Leutnant Rüdiger von Kirchmayr. An Austrian and the *Staffelkapitän* of 5. *Staffel*, von Kirchmayr was an experienced pilot who had served as Technical Officer of his parent *Gruppe* in early 1943. Despite being shot down and wounded flying an Fw 190A-5 in aerial combat over Aachen on 1 December 1943, he ended that year credited with at least six victories.

Ordered aloft from Rheine in an *Alarmstart*, von Kirchmayr led II./JG 1 in the direction of the approaching bombers in his Fw 190A-7 Wk-Nr 430172 'Black 1'. Directed by radio, he and his comrades in his *Kette* (Leutnant Fritz Wegner and Feldwebel Sauer) spotted a formation of '50–60' B-17s at 6300m over the western edge of the Harz mountains at 1126 hrs. Von Kirchmayr ordered the *Gruppe* to make two tightly formed frontal attacks from out of the sun against the lead *Pulk* of some 20 bombers. This done, the Focke-Wulfs assembled for a second attack, and von Kirchmayr selected the extreme outer-flying B-17 to the right of the formation. He opened fire from 600m directly ahead of the target, and later reported:

After making a tight *Gruppe* frontal attack, I launched a second tight attack on the lead group of about 20 B-17s. Coming out of the sun, I opened fired at the Boeing flying on the right and to the front at the same height and from 600m, closing into the minimum range. Pieces from the cockpit and individual parts of the fuselage and wings flew away, whereupon the Boeing extended its landing gear and spiralled downwards to the right.

After the *Gruppe's* two attacks, I led a third frontal attack. Due to a slight change in course by the Boeing formation, I had to launch the attack at an angle of 15–20 degrees from the front right side and at the same height. Approaching from out of the sun, I fired at the Boeing flying in the lead group of about 20 B-17s of the top right flight and was able to observe hits in the left inner engine, which trailed a thick plume of black smoke. The ball turret and individual parts of the cockpit, fuselage and wings flew away. The Boeing lagged behind the formation and slowly gave up altitude.

Von Kirchmayr's second victim was seen to crash two to four kilometres southwest of Osterode, although he was credited with the destruction of only one bomber for his sixth victory. In the space of minutes, II./JG 1 claimed ten B-17s shot down, another as a *Herausschuss* and one probable. In return, Unteroffizier Erwin Mietho of 6./JG 1 was killed and a pilot from 5. *Staffel* wounded.

Aside from *Sturmstaffel* 1 and the three *Gruppen* of JG 1, *Gruppen* from JG 11, JG 26, JG 27, JG 54, JG 300, JG 302 and *Zerstörergeschwader* (ZG) 26, plus some nightfighter units, were in action – a total of 579 aircraft. The USAAF reported the loss of 65 bombers and eight fighters, while the Luftwaffe lost 58 aircraft, with 38 crew killed and 28 wounded.

A large-scale raid was planned against Frankfurt-am-Main on 24 January, but bad weather forced VIII Bomber Command to recall its aircraft. This resulted in considerable confusion and bomber formations becoming broken up. Despite the inclement weather, a small force of Fw 190s from 1./JG 1 led by the *Staffelkapitän*, Hauptmann Alfred Grislawski, was scrambled from Oldenburg. A recipient of the Knight's Cross, Grislawski had been credited with his 120th victory on the 11th, the same day that von Kirchmayr had downed a B-17.

Once airborne, 1./JG 1 linked up with the rest of I. *Gruppe* and *Sturmstaffel* 1. The Focke-Wulfs intercepted B-17s of the 13th Combat Wing (CW) over Belgium, managing to evade the escort which was committed against fighters from other German units. Grislawski approached the lead bomber box from behind and targeted a B-17 in the lead box of the 95th Bombardment Group (BG) at about 8000m. He opened fire. Seconds later, SSgt Harvey Kreitzman, the flight engineer in B-17F 42-30181 *HERKY JERKY II* of the 335th Bombardment Squadron (BS), glanced up into the top gun turret, which he saw 'resembled a spider's web, shot to smithereens'. Kreitzman quickly moved to fire his guns, but saw Grislawski's Focke-Wulf diving past out of view. He also noticed that *HERKY JERKY II's* huge tail fin was missing.

Grislawski had observed a large explosion just forward of the Flying Fortress's tail fin. The bomber was on fire, its tail gone, and over the intercom its pilot, 2Lt Clay Burnett, shouted at his crew to bail out. As he banked past and away, Grislawski felt defensive fire from the B-17 thump into his aircraft. The bomber was trailing flames, but a second later the tail section of Grislawski's Focke-Wulf also broke away and his fighter went into a half-roll. Under the G-forces, the German ace blacked out as his machine entered a flat spin through the clouds. Recovering consciousness and fighting a blasting wind, Grislawski somehow

Hauptmann Alfred Grislawski, *Staffelkapitän* of 1./JG 1, watches a mechanic work on his Fw 190A-7 at Dortmund in January 1944. The aircraft carries the winged '1' emblem of JG 1, and both the area under the engine as well as the rear fuselage identification band are in the *Geschwader* colour of red. The engine-mounted machine guns have been fitted with flame suppressors. Grislawski had claimed 127 victories (14 of them four-engined bombers) by war's end. (EN Archive)

managed to extricate himself from the Fw 190, smacking his head against the wing and badly grazing his leg. With the aid of his parachute, he was able to land safely in the snow-covered Belgian countryside, and later on, while recovering in hospital, he met the wounded ball turret gunner of the B-17 he had shot down.

Continuing its *Pointblank* goal of 'undermining the morale of the German people to a point where their capacity for armed resistance is fatally weakened', the Eighth Air Force sent 777 heavy bombers to target aircraft manufacturing plants around Braunschweig and Hannover on 30 January. Escorted by 635 fighters, the bombers were again forced to bomb through cloud.

At 1145 hrs, accompanied by *Sturmstaffel* 1, I./JG 1 made contact with a large formation of *Viermots* southwest of Osnabrück. The *Sturmstaffel* separated from the main German force and closed in on a formation of B-24s – probably the 39 aircraft of the 1st CW which had diverted towards Hannover due to dense smoke and contrails encountered over Braunschweig. One Liberator fell to the guns of Unteroffizier Willi Maximowitz for his first aerial victory, while in conformity with the oath he had taken, Unteroffizier Hermann Wahlfeld rammed another, remarkably without any injury to himself.

Leutnant Richard Franz of *Sturmstaffel* 1 recalled:

At that time *Sturmstaffel* 1 was the only unit which attacked the *Viermots* from the rear, and all the other pilots who flew in the *Reichsverteidigung* thought we were a little bit crazy. They all preferred to attack head-on, with the advantages and disadvantages that came with it. The *Sturmstaffel* pilots, on the other hand, voluntarily bound themselves to bring down one bomber per engagement, either with their weapons or by ramming. I never had to ram, thank God.

I./JG 1 reported the destruction of seven B-17s for the loss of four Fw 190s and three pilots. *Sturmstaffel* 1 suffered the loss of Fahnrich Manfred Derp from defensive fire west of Osnabrück and also, in a cruel irony, Unteroffizier Heinz

Unteroffizier Willi Maximowitz of *Sturmstaffel* 1 sits in the cockpit of his Fw 190A-6 'White 10' at Salzwedel in early 1944. Note the damage to the armoured glass canopy panel and to the fuselage just above the aircraft's tactical number, likely caused by defensive fire from a bomber during a close-range attack or from the fire from an American fighter. Such damage justified the fitment of additional side protection even at the cost of manoeuvrability. (EN Archive)

von Neuenstein, who had promised his father that he would 'do his duty' in his letter home a few days before. Leutnant Ulrich Blaese was wounded and forced to bail out of his Fw 190 near Diepholz. It would be a long time before he was again fit for operations. Unteroffizier Werner Peinemann suffered burns to his face and hands before taking to his parachute not far from Sachsenhagen. Unlike Blaese, however, Peinemann was back in action within a few weeks.

This early combat experience, combined with the highly hazardous nature of their work, may have served as the motivation behind some *Sturmstaffel* pilots experimenting with the wearing of steel infantry helmets as a form of additional armour protection during the initial period of operations. Feldwebel Oscar Bösch remembered his fellow pilots telling him, 'It, not surprisingly, proved impractical. Wearing a steel helmet in the cockpit resulted in the complete inability of the pilot to move his head when in combat!' The idea was soon abandoned.

Despite a failed attempt to form a *Gefechtsverband* with the Fw 190s of I./JG 11, at 1030 hrs on 10 February I./JG 1 and *Sturmstaffel* 1 took off and, together with II./JG 1, were directed to attack the 169 B-17s of the 3rd BD heading for the aircraft plants around Braunschweig. The German formation was led by Major Heinz Bär, who had been appointed the *Kapitän* of 6. *Staffel* the month before. Bär was one of the Luftwaffe's most experienced and accomplished fighter pilots with a service career that stretched back to 1939, the year he scored his first victory in the West. In the Soviet Union in August 1941, he was awarded the Oak Leaves to the Knight's Cross for shooting down six aircraft in one day. With his score of aerial victories standing at 90, Bär was

The *Gruppenkommandeur* of II./JG 1, Major Heinz Bär, inspects B-17F 42-3040 *MISS OUACHITA* of the 323rd BS/91st BG which he shot down while flying an Fw 190 on 21 February 1944 – he claimed two Flying Fortresses and a P-51 destroyed on this date, taking his tally to 178 victories. Damage can be seen to the leading edge of the bomber's tail assembly, and the root to the port wing has been ripped open on impact with the ground. Nevertheless, in this condition, the aircraft would have provided Luftwaffe airmen and engineers with valuable technical intelligence. (EN Archive)

decorated with the Swords on 16 February 1942. Leaving the Eastern Front three months later, he was given command of I./JG 77, with whom he flew over the Mediterranean, claiming another 45 victories despite contracting a bout of malaria and being stricken by gastric ulcers.

In the summer of 1943 Bär was transferred to France, where he took over command of the operational training unit *Jagdgruppe Süd*. Ill and exhausted from combat, he returned to Germany for a period of convalescence, before embarking on a long stint as one of the foremost unit commanders in the defence of the Reich. His plain speaking on tactical policies did not enamour him to Göring, however, who saw fit to 'demote' him. Thus Bär's next posting was to 11./JG 1 at Volkel, in the Netherlands, as a *Staffelführer*, but he was soon posted to 6./JG 1 at Rheine.

During the 10 February raid the USAAF bombers were protected by 466 P-38, P-47 and P-51 fighters, and the day would see some of the hardest-fought aerial combat ever to take place over northwest Europe.

Major Bär guided his fighters for an attack on the bombers north of Osnabrück. Thirteen B-17s were claimed as brought down by JG 1, including one credited to Bär, as well as a P-47, representing his 180th and 181st victories. Tenacity and an undeniable combat record meant that by the time of the great air battles over Berlin in March 1944, Bär was once again entrusted with more senior command, and appointed *Kommandeur* of II./JG 1 upon the death of the previous incumbent, Hauptmann Hermann Seegatz, who had been killed in action during the raid on the German capital on 6 March.

In late February, the Eighth Air Force launched Operation *Argument* or 'Big Week', a concerted and intense bombing campaign against German aircraft production centres commencing on the 20th. Bombers specifically targeted the principal airframe, final assembly and component plants at Leipzig-Mockau, Halberstadt and Regensburg that were responsible for the output of single-

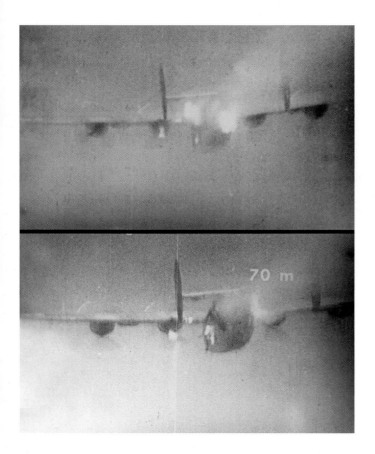

Gun camera stills depict the moment an Fw 190 closes to within 70m of a B-24 Liberator during a rear attack. (Author's Collection)

and twin-engined fighter aircraft. The offensive was intended to do two things – destroy German aircraft on the ground and the means of replacing them, and force the Luftwaffe into the air to defend against attacks mounted on vital installations. In all, 16 Combat Wings of heavy bombers totalling 1000 aircraft were committed to the operation, together with fighter protection from all available fighter groups in both the Eighth and Ninth Air Forces. It was to be the largest force ever assembled in the history of American strategic air power.

The Luftwaffe showed its teeth intermittently. Following its mission to Gotha on 24 February, the 2nd BD reported its B-24 Liberators as 'being attacked almost the entire period over Germany.' It seemed that the Luftwaffe fighters had gained a new confidence, the Fw 190s of JG 1 and JG 26 'pressing home vicious nose attacks', whilst elsewhere, 'some groups were forced far off course, and these formations and especially stragglers were attacked unceasingly.' That day, the 2nd BD alone lost 33 four-engined bombers.

However, to counter any sense of achievement, the losses in February were devastating, and included more valued aces and recipients of the Knight's Cross. Hauptmann Egon Mayer, the *Kommodore* of JG 2 who, as mentioned in the previous chapter, was a key tactician in the war against the bombers, as well as the first pilot to accumulate 100 victories solely on the Channel Front, fell prey to American fighters. Mayer's loss was especially hard to bear, since he had become the highest scorer against the bombers with 25 *Viermots* to his credit. Others were to follow.

Following the 'Big Week' attacks, the USAAF felt sufficiently confident to concentrate their efforts on Berlin in a series of raids known to participating crews as 'Big-B' missions. The German capital was the 'hub' of the Third Reich's war effort, housing the administrative and ministerial headquarters of all three armed services. It was also a major rail centre, with 12 main lines meeting there from various directions.

The first strike was mounted on 4 March when a force of 500 B-17s and B-24s escorted by 770 fighters headed for the capital. The concept behind the 'Big-B' missions was not solely to bomb the important industrial targets of Berlin, nor even to dent civilian morale, but rather it was an attempt to coax Luftwaffe fighters into the air so as to inflict further unsustainable losses. The Eighth Air Force's trump card was the P-51B Mustang. Equipped with twin 108-US gallon wing tanks, the fighter was now able to escort the bombers as far as the capital. Fortunately for the city, however, adverse weather conditions prevented all but 30 aircraft from one Combat Wing of the 3rd BD from reaching their primary target, where the bombers duly unloaded 68 tons of ordnance but inflicted little damage.

Sturmstaffel 1 had taken off from Salzwedel at 1230 hrs on a southerly course. Having searched the skies for an hour, the unit wheeled to the north and intercepted the American bombers near Neuruppin. Closing in from behind, and ignoring the defensive fire from the B-17s, the *Sturmstaffel* pilots opened up with their MK 108 cannon at just a few metres from their targets. The result was devastating. Feldwebel Hermann Wahlfeld shot down two bombers, flying through his victims' debris, and Unteroffizier Gerhard Vivroux also shot down a B-17. However, Feldwebel Walter Peinemann was shot down and wounded between Neuruppin and Salzwedel and a further Fw 190 was damaged.

Major Erwin Bacsila of *Sturmstaffel* 1 prepares to jump from the cockpit of his Fw 190A-6 at Salzwedel in late January 1944. Note the additional armoured glass side panels fitted to the canopy and the armoured panel added to the side of the cockpit just below Bacsila's boots. (EN Archive)

On the 6th, VIII Bomber Command mounted a second attempt on Berlin, and this time it succeeded in reaching the German capital in large numbers. The Eighth Air Force despatched 504 B-17s and 226 B-24s to strike at industrial targets around the city, escorted by a record 801 fighters drawn from 17 groups. However, heavy cloud meant that 474 B-17s and 198 B-24s bombed their secondary targets and targets of opportunity in the city itself through breaks in the cloud cover.

The Luftwaffe had been expecting the raid and had prepared itself by practising, several days before, the assembly of large *Gefechtsverbände* over Lake Steinhuder northwest of Hannover in an attempt to meet mass with mass. So it was that on this day no fewer than 19 *Jagdgruppen*, three *Zerstörergruppen* and four *Nachtjagdgruppen*, together with a handful of miscellaneous units, were available to take on the *Viermots*.

Leutnant Richard Franz of *Sturmstaffel* 1 recalled:

Normally, we were informed at about 0700 hrs of a '*grosse Versammlung*' [large enemy assembly] over Great Yarmouth. After breakfast, we were driven to the *Staffel*'s dispersal and then had 30 minutes readiness. About 45 minutes before the expected take-off, and after determination of the probable target area, cockpit readiness was ordered until finally the scramble order was given. After scrambling, all units were ordered to meet at a certain point and then form up into a battle formation – sometimes up to 100 aircraft – before being directed to a pre-assigned attack position from where we would separate from the main formation for our rearward attack. The main formation would always try to overtake the bomber stream in order to get into position for a head-on attack.

The first B-17s reached the Dutch coastline at 1052 hrs. With engines running at cruising speed to conserve fuel, the escort fighters slowly made up the distance between themselves and their charges.

At last, the interminable *Sitzbereitschaft* came to an end on the majority of Luftwaffe fighter bases across western Europe. At Twente, in the Netherlands, Major Schnoor's I./JG 1 took off at 1055 hrs, setting course for Lake Steinhuder. I. *Gruppe* was joined over Rheine by the 21 Fw 190s of II./JG 1, led by Major Bär. The two *Gruppen* were the last to reach the lake, meeting up with 50 Bf 109s and Fw 190s from JG 11, and 20 Bf 109s of III./JG 54. JG 1's arrival meant that more than 100 fighters would go into action – a force which far exceeded the usual German strike capability. However, their numbers could still not compare with those put into the fray by the Americans.

The debris of around ten Flying Fortresses fell in the Quackenbrück area. But it was then the turn of the German fighters to become boxed in as slowly but surely the escort reacted. One of the first victims was the Fw 190 of 19-victory ace Oberleutnant Wolfgang Kretschmer, recently arrived from JG 54, who lost contact with the rest of II. *Gruppe* after probably having shot down a *Viermot* during the frontal attack.

Alone, Kretschmer was preparing for a second attack from the rear. At full throttle, ace Col Hubert 'Hub' Zemke, commander of the 56th FG, flew his P-47 towards Kretschmer. The latter realised the gravity of his situation too late, and despite his frantic evasive manoeuvres, Kretschmer could not escape. The American opened fire, the Focke-Wulf's fuselage was hit and the aircraft began to break up and burn. Blinded by the flames and deafened by the noise around him, Kretschmer managed to extricate himself with difficulty from the spiralling inferno. Finally clear, the shock of the parachute opening brought home to him that he was still alive. He was later found on the ground, his face, hands and clothing ravaged by flames. An ambulance took Kretschmer away for treatment, and he subsequently spent ten weeks in convalescence in Quackenbrück. High above, the action continued.

Shortly after 1130 hrs, seven Fw 190s from *Sturmstaffel* 1 joined the Bf 109s of IV./JG 3 as they took off from Salzwedel and headed towards Magdeburg, where they were due to form up with units drawn from 1. and 7. *Jagddivisionen* and placed under the command of Major Hans Kogler, *Kommandeur* of III./ZG 26. Rendezvous was made at an altitude of 8000m near Magdeburg. Once assembled, this large *Gefechtsverband* comprised a lead element of *Zerstörer*, many equipped with underwing batteries of four W.Gr.21 mortars intended to break up the approaching enemy formation. Behind the *Zerstörer* came a force of 72 Bf 109s and Fw 190s from I., II. and IV./JG 3, *Sturmstaffel* 1, JG 302 and the *Jasta Erla* works defence flight.

Towards 1230 hrs, the enemy bombers were sighted – 112 B-17s of the 1st and 94th CWs of the 1st BD. The twin-engined heavy fighters went in first and fired off their mortars. As they did so, P-51s dived out of the sun to intercept them, and in doing so forced the *Zerstörer* pilots to break off their attacks early. The result was that many of the mortars exploded way off target.

For *Sturmstaffel* 1, it was to be the most successful day since the unit's formation. Moving in to attack from the rear, the *Staffel* closed in on B-17s of the 91st BG. Unteroffizier Kurt Röhrich scored his third victory at 1235 hrs, together with Unteroffizier Willi Maximowitz, who claimed a *Herausschuss*, and Leutnant Gerhard Dost, who registered his first victory. Three minutes later, Feldwebel Hermann Wahlfeld, who had shot down two bombers two days before, added to his personal score when he recorded his third victory. Oberleutnant Othmar Zehart followed at 1255 hrs when he scored his second victory. Following his success, Leutnant Dost was killed in his Fw 190A-7 'White 20' while attempting to escape two P-51s near Salzwedel.

One Focke-Wulf of *Sturmstaffel* 1 collided with B-17G 42-31432 *My Darling Also* of the 401st BS/91st BG. The Fw 190 descended slightly as it approached and took hits, but then climbed 'relentlessly' towards *My Darling Also*. The latter was already badly damaged by fire from the German fighter, which hit the Boeing bomber and knocked away its entire right stabiliser. The B-17 fell away out of control. Eight crew were subsequently killed and two bailed out and were taken prisoner. In a post-mission report, the 1st BD described the attack on the 1st and 94th CWs as 'vicious'.

In what appears to be a staged photograph, overseen by a senior NCO, an Fw 190A-7 of I./JG 11 undergoes servicing and re-arming during an instructional session at Rotenburg in March 1944. A cable leads from the generator plug-in socket in the rear fuselage while the aircraft's fuel tanks are also replenished. Armourers prepare to load ammunition into the outer wing MG 151/20. (EN Archive)

Although B-24J Liberator 42-7586 *God Bless Our Ship* of the 701st BS/445th BG was hit by Flak over Berlin on 6 March 1944, this scene is typical of a heavy bomber that force-landed in German-held territory. Here, Luftwaffe personnel are in the process of inspecting the aircraft and removing any items of technical interest at the crash site some 40km north of the German capital. (Author's Collection)

In what may have been a second mission intended to attack the bombers on their return run, the *Sturmstaffel's* Leutnant Werner Gerth claimed his second and third victories at 1405 hrs and 1408 hrs, respectively.

In all, by the time the *Gefechtsverband* broke off its attack, having expended both fuel and ammunition, eight B-17s had been shot down and three more destroyed in collisions. Four P-51 escort fighters also went down in the Berlin area. However, for the Germans, the price of this 'success' was high. In total, the Luftwaffe suffered 87 single- or twin-engined fighters lost or damaged on 6 March, with 36 aircrew killed and 27 wounded. Among those lost was Leutnant Hugo Frey, *Staffelkapitän* of 7./JG 11, who had claimed four bombers destroyed that day prior to being shot down and killed near Sleen, in the Netherlands. These successes took his tally to 32 victories, including 26 four-engined, and Frey would be awarded the Knight's Cross posthumously.

On the American side, 53 B-17s and 16 B-24s failed to return, 293 B-17s and 54 B-24s were damaged and five B-17s and one B-24 written off. Seventeen crew were killed, 31 wounded and 686 listed as missing. Aside from the damage caused by the bombers, their presence in the skies over Berlin had a huge psychological impact on the Germans. Their capital could no longer be considered immune from attack, no longer out of range of USAAF heavy bombers. The pressure on the pilots of the *Sturmstaffel* and the other outnumbered fighter units operating in the defence of the Reich could only intensify as a result.

On 23 March, 707 B-17s and B-24s headed for the cities of Braunschweig and Münster and the airfields at Achmer and Handorf – all secondary targets and targets of opportunity due to bad weather. Shortly before 1000 hrs, *Sturmstaffel* 1, together with aircraft from IV./JG 3, took off from Salzwedel and set off for Magdeburg, where they rendezvoused at 1015 hrs with Bf 109Gs from II./JG 3. Once assembled into a *Gefechtsverband*, this force then headed west towards an area southeast of Münster. The *Sturmstaffel* was led by its commander, Major von Kornatzki, who apparently only flew a few combat sorties.

At 1100 hrs, contact was made with the 296 B-17s of the 1st BD that were flying due west, having bombed their target at Münster. They were covered by a heavy escort of P-51 Mustangs. The German formation overflew the bomber *Pulk* from the left, wheeled ahead and at 1120 hrs, from north of Hamm, launched a massed frontal attack. Within the space of ten minutes, *Sturmstaffel* 1 accounted for six B-17s shot down or forced out of formation. Von Kornatzki claimed a *Herausschuss* for his fifth victory, as did Leutnant Friedrich Dammann at 1117 hrs for his first score. Other bombers were shot down by Unteroffiziere Gerhard Vivroux and Kurt Röhrich, Flieger Wolfgang Kosse and Unteroffizier Willi Maximowitz, who downed a B-17 over his home town of Wuppertal. The latter was hit while attacking the bomber, and he had to perform an emergency landing near Wuppertal.

The *Sturmstaffel's* success against the bombers on 23 March surpassed the efforts of IV./JG 3, which sent four B-17s and one P-51 down. However, it was not without cost – Feldwebel Wahlfeld, who had rammed a bomber in January, went down near Lippstadt and Feldwebel Otto Weissenberger was killed near Nordick (Heiden).

Throughout April 1944, the American bomber offensive ground on, targeting aircraft production plants in central and southern Germany, while Eighth Air Force fighter escorts, as well as tactical fighters of the Ninth Air Force, began to strafe German airfields. The skies over the Fatherland were no longer safe for the *Jagdwaffe*.

Mechanics take a break to enjoy a cigarette on the wing of an Fw 190A-7 of *Sturmstaffel* 1 at Salzwedel in April 1944. The Focke-Wulf bears the black-white-black rear fuselage band of the *Sturmstaffel*. (EN Archive)

On 8 April fog prevented a large part of the 1st BD from taking off to attack its assigned airfield target at Oldenburg. The 3rd BD despatched 255 B-17s to airfields across northwest Germany and the B-24s of the 2nd BD headed for aircraft plants at Braunschweig, as well as Langenhagen airfield and other targets. The whole force was protected by 780 fighters. In response, at 1250 hrs, Major Bär's II./JG 1, which had moved its 45 Fw 190s and a single Bf 109 from Rheine to Störmede, 11km southeast of Lippstadt, during the first week of April, was given the *Alarmstart* and 36 Focke-Wulfs took off to rendezvous with I. and III. *Gruppen*.

Ordered towards Brocken, the *Gruppe* sighted a formation of approximately 300 B-17s and B-24s with around 30–40 escorts on its inbound course between Braunschweig and Magdeburg shortly after 1330 hrs. Twenty minutes later, II./JG 1 made a mass attack on a formation of some 50 Liberators of the 2nd BD from ahead and below. Bär scored first, knocking a B-24 down at 1350 hrs for his 198th victory, while Oberleutnant Georg-Peter Eder, commanding 6. *Staffel*, scored a minute later for his 34th victory when he targeted one of two bombers flying to the outer right-hand side of the *Pulk*. He observed hits in the fuselage and starboard wing before the Liberator burst into flames, falling away from its formation. The bomber impacted southwest of Salzwedel.

The redoubtable 'Schorsch' Eder had once flown as *Staffelkapitän* of 12./JG 2, where, in late 1942, he had been instrumental in working with Hauptmann Egon Mayer to develop the principle of the head-on attack against four-engined bombers. Despite being shot down and wounded in the Soviet Union, as well as having suffering a fractured skull following a collision on the ground with a Ju 52/3m whilst on the Eastern Front, Eder quickly proved his abilities in this new form of warfare in the West when he shot down a B-17 on 30 December 1942, with another following four days later.

Whilst taking his tally of Flying Fortresses destroyed to five on 28 March 1943, Eder's Bf 109G-4 was hit in the engine by defensive fire and his fighter somersaulted upon landing. The ace was injured once again, taking him off operations for several weeks. By 14 July 1943, Eder had claimed eight B-17s destroyed, and on that day, during Eighth Air Force raids on German airfields in France, he shot down two more during the early morning. On 5 November Eder again had to take to his parachute following combat. In March 1944, after commanding 5./JG 2, he was posted to 6./JG 1, his victory score standing at 33, including 11 B-17s.

Barely a minute after Eder claimed his victim on 8 April, one of his *Staffel*'s pilots, Feldwebel Wolfgang Brunner, leading a *Rotte* in his Fw 190A-7 Wk-Nr 340280 'Yellow 6', achieved a dramatic kill 7000m above the countryside to the southwest of Salzwedel:

As the *Gruppe* turned in to attack the Liberator *Pulk*, on a frontal pass I fired two bursts from a distance of 600m, closing to 200m, at a Liberator flying to the right and in the centre of the *Pulk*. After the second burst, the Liberator started to burn at the rear of the fuselage while still flying in formation with its wing still attached. Then the burning fuselage fell perpendicularly to the ground. I was unable to observed the crash impact due to the fighter defence.

This was Brunner's second victory, and he expended 200 mixed rounds of incendiary and armour-piercing ammunition from his MG 131s and 240 similar rounds from his MG 151/20s.

In the space of just two minutes, II./JG 1 shot down nine B-24s. Altogether, the 2nd BD lost 30 Liberators to enemy action that day.

A *Gefechtsverband* comprising *Sturmstaffel* 1 and *Stab*, I., II. and IV./JG 3 was sent up to intercept more bombers from the 2nd BD northwest of Braunschweig. Launching a massed frontal attack over Fallersleben, the German fighters soon became embroiled in a large aerial battle with P-51s and P-38s as the B-24s commenced their bomb run. The *Sturmstaffel* engaged a box of Liberators, and within a matter of minutes it had shot down four of them. Unteroffizier Kurt Röhrich claimed his fifth victory, Leutnant Siegfried Müller his third, Unteroffizier Heinz Steffen a *Herausschuss*, representing his third victory, and Leutnant Richard Franz his third. Franz remembered:

Fw 190A-8/R2 Wk-Nr 681513 'Yellow 12' of 6.(*Sturm*)/JG 300 at Finsterwalde has been fitted with cockpit side armour. The pilot seen with his aircraft is Fahnenjunker-Oberfeldwebel Lothar Födisch, who was killed on 7 October 1944. (EN Archive).

After this mission, I had the opportunity to meet a crew member of the bomber I had shot down. I landed at Magdeburg airfield and met him there in the operations

DOWNING *OL' DOG*

This dramatic artwork shows the early afternoon clash of 29 May 1944 between an Fw 190A-8 of 11.(*Sturm*)/JG 3, possibly flown by Unteroffizier Karl-Heinz Schmidt, and B-17G 42-31924 *OL' DOG* of the 344th BS/95th BG. The Flying Fortress, from the 3rd BD, had earlier been shot up by a formation of Fw 190s as the bomber neared its target of Leipzig. The attack had left the Plexiglas nose of the B-17 shattered, its No. 2 engine with a windmilling propeller and the left rear stabiliser in tatters.

As he returned to his base at Salzwedel, having attacked other 3rd BD Flying Fortresses, Schmidt, accompanied by another Fw 190, chanced upon the now 'straggling' *OL' DOG*, already flying at low-level. One of the Focke-Wulfs made a head-on attack, opening fire as it approached the Flying Fortress. As the pilot of the B-17, 2Lt Norman A. Ulrich, dived towards tree-top level, the first of the Fw 190s swept to the right, over the nose of *OL' DOG*, and passed above its starboard wing. The second Fw 190 then commenced an attack from the side, but broke off. The two fighters remained with the stricken enemy bomber until it force-landed in a field near Packebusch. Unteroffizier Schmidt was officially credited with the *'endgültige Vernichtung'* (final destruction) of a B-17 at 1322 hrs. This did not count towards his eventual tally of six confirmed aerial victories, however.

FOLLOWING PAGES

room. He was a lieutenant, his name was Andy and he was the only member of the crew who had survived the attack. We had a good talk, and he presented me with his flying jacket – half leather and half silk, with 24 previous missions written in ink on the silk part of the jacket, including the date and target. He told me that this was their last mission and that, had they returned, they would have been posted back to the States. But he also felt lucky to be alive. I had that jacket until the end of the war, when I was shot down for the last time on 25 April 1945 by a Russian fighter over Berlin.

Three days later, on 11 April, the USAAF attempted a maximum effort when it despatched a record-breaking force of 917 B-17s and B-24s to bomb aircraft plants at Poznan, Sorau, Bernburg, Halberstadt, Stettin, Cottbus and Oschersleben. The bombers came with 800 escort fighters drawn from both the Eighth and Ninth Air Forces, although with VIII Bomber Command stretching its resources over such a wide range of deep penetration targets, even this escort was barely adequate. The Luftwaffe's three northern fighter divisions put up 432 single- and twin-engined fighters in response.

At 1005 hrs, *Sturmstaffel* 1 and IV./JG 3 received the *Alarmstart* and took off from Salzwedel to form up into a *Gefechtsverband* with elements of various units drawn from 1. and 3. *Jagddivisionen*. The American bombers were sighted some 40 minutes later between Braunschweig and Halberstadt. The Fw 190s of *Sturmstaffel* 1 separated from the Bf 109G-6s of IV./JG 3, with the latter unit directing its attack against a combat box of B-17s, whilst the former closed in on a formation of some 50 B-24s from the 2nd BD in the Hildesheim area.

For the Americans it was to be carnage, whilst the *Sturmstaffel* enjoyed the most successful action in its short-lived history. In one pass, five B-24s were either shot down or cut away from their formation in 60 seconds thanks to the efforts of Leutnante Rudolf Metz (second victory), Werner Gerth (fourth) and Siegfried Müller (fourth), Oberfeldwebel Gerhard Marburg (third) and Unteroffizier Kurt Röhrich (sixth, *Herausschuss*). Two minutes later, Marburg claimed a *Herausschuss*, while Gerth downed another B-24. Röhrich also accounted for one of the P-47 escorts – the first fighter to be shot down by the *Sturmstaffel*.

USAAF post-mission reports made no mention of German attacks mounted from the rear, and it may have been that on this occasion the *Sturmstaffel* attacked from the front in mass formation with the other units involved.

Following this action, a few *Sturmjäger*, together with elements of IV./JG 3, joined up and flew in formation back to Salzwedel. Once landed, they quickly refuelled and rearmed for a second mission directed against the returning bombers. They took off at 1240 hrs. Heading to the northwest, it took them only 15 minutes to find their prey. Thirty minutes later, having assembled into attack position, the *Sturmjäger* closed in on a formation of B-17s, most probably from the 3rd BD, returning from bombing Rostock and Stettin. Unteroffizier Vivroux of *Sturmstaffel* 1 shot down a B-17 (his third victory) at 1318 hrs, whilst pilots of IV./JG 3 claimed nine more.

According to the Eighth Air Force, the Luftwaffe performed 'one of its most severe and well co-ordinated defences marked by skilful handling of a considerable number of twin-engined day fighters in the Stettin area and single-engine fighters in the Hannover-Oschersleben area.'

Between Hannover and Oschersleben lay Fallersleben, an outlying district of Wolfsburg, and it would be over the countryside north of Fallersleben that II./JG 1 would once again clash with B-17s. Their pilots already at cockpit readiness at Störmede, the *Gruppe's* 24 Focke-Wulfs were led aloft at 0958 hrs by Major Bär in his Fw 190A-7 'Red 23'. They were directed to assemble with I. and III./JG 1 over Paderborn and Bad Lippspringe, with further instructions to form a *Gefechtsverband* to the east, over Brocken, with elements of JG 27 flying Bf 109s as high cover. However, the latter rendezvous failed because of confusion in communications between the 2. and 3. *Jagddivisionen*, and so JG 1 pressed on on a northwesterly course. As they approached Fallersleben, some 15–18 Flying Fortresses were spotted flying a northeasterly course at 7000m under escort from around 40 P-51s and P-47s. Bär reported:

The *Gruppe* turned left and carried out a formation attack from the front. I targeted the B-17 flying lowest in a small *Pulk* from the front and below and scored hits in the fuselage and cabin, whereupon the B-17 immediately began to trail light-coloured smoke. As I passed through [the bomber formation], I observed that the Boeing veered over vertically on its left wing. I was not able to observe the impact crash as further combat ensued with enemy fighters.

It was 1059 hrs, and the B-17 would be claimed as Bär's 199th aerial victory. A minute later, fellow ace Oberleutnant Georg-Peter Eder, leading 6./JG 1, struck again whilst flying Fw 190A-7 Wk-Nr 430645 'Yellow 4':

0842 hrs, 8 MAY 1944

NIENBURG

1 At 0842 hrs, Fw 190s of IV.(*Sturm*)/JG 3, together with the *Geschwaderstab* and the former aircraft and pilots of *Sturmstaffel* 1, make contact with the B-24s of the 2nd BD's 445th BG, heading for Braunschweig.

2 Mistaken for American aircraft while flying at 3000m alongside the Liberators, some of the Fw 190s are targeted by friendly Flak. Feldwebel Oscar Bösch's aircraft is hit in the engine. Oil sprays onto his windscreen, and, trailing smoke behind him, he leaves the formation and turns into the path of the bombers.

3 Protected from enemy fire as he dives through some 60+ bombers, Bösch aims at the last B-24 and opens fire.

4 Hit with the full force of the Fw 190's cannon, the Liberator bursts into flames (and eventually explodes) as Bösch veers hard away from his victim and attempts to make another attack.

5 With his ammunition expended, Bösch decides to ram the next bomber in line. Slanting in from an angle, he hits its slipstream and misses the B-24, passing very close to his intended target.

6 With the entire bomber formation now firing at his departing fighter, Bösch is cloaked by defensive fire. Pushing his control column forward, Bösch makes good his escape by diving steeply away at 1000km/h in the stricken Fw 190 before bailing out at 6000m.

FOLLOWING PAGES

The *Gruppe* made an immediate close formation frontal attack. During this attack I fired at the right wing of a Boeing, from forward and below, closing from 600m to 100m, with further bursts. The Boeing received strikes in the fuselage and blew apart during my attack. I could not observe the individual pieces as they fell vertically to the ground for I was attacked by enemy fighters and had to turn to attack them.

This became Eder's 37th victory.

As referenced by Bär and Eder, after the *Gruppe's* pass through the bombers, due to the strength of the fighter escort it was not possible to reassemble for a second attack, and the subsequent combat broke down into individual engagements fought at *Rotte* and *Schwarm*-strength. By the time II./JG 1 returned to Störmede, it had shot down seven bombers in 60 seconds, including an unconfirmed kill to Oberleutnant Eberhard Burath. Four pilots were lost to the escort fighters, and when the *Gruppe* returned to base the pilots were dismayed to discover that it had been attacked by four P-47s that had left six Fw 190s destroyed, two more damaged and five personnel wounded.

On 29 April OKL redesignated IV./JG 3 as a new *Sturmgruppe* under the command of Hauptmann Wilhelm Moritz, becoming IV.(*Sturm*)/JG 3. The new *Gruppe* was to be re-equipped solely with, as the OKL directive described it, '*Sturm-Flugzeuge Fw 190*'. *Sturmstaffel* 1 was dissolved, and its pilots and groundcrew formed the nucleus of 11.(*Sturm*)/JG 3 under the command of Leutnant Werner Gerth.

On 8 May the USAAF returned to Berlin and Braunschweig. Nearly 750 B-17s and B-24s, escorted by more than 729 fighters, reached Germany, with the Liberators of the 2nd BD leading the formation on a straight route to Berlin, passing over the Zuider Zee and onwards, north of Hannover. East of Uelzen, the 2nd BD, together with the 45th CW from the 3rd BD which had become separated from the Berlin force, turned south to bomb Braunschweig.

At 0842 hrs, IV.(*Sturm*)/JG 3 and *Stab*/JG 3 were airborne to intercept. At 1000 hrs, despite worsening weather, contact was made with the B-24s. One of the pilots to engage the Liberators was Feldwebel Oscar Bösch:

I particularly remember the 8 May mission, the details of which are engraved in my memory for it went wrong from the beginning. We were flying at 3000m beside a box of B-24s at a slightly lower altitude when our own Flak mistook us for a target! A shell exploded near my Fw 190 and riddled it with shrapnel. Almost immediately, a trail of oil appeared on my windshield and hood. An oil pipe had been hit. I called on the radio to my comrades that I had to leave the flight. This I did without losing a minute, getting closer and closer to the B-24s. As I flew my aircraft down through the bomber formation, I found that I had to fire at the last B-24, which burst into fragments. I continued to fire as I flew through the formation, but I had no time to observe the results because in a brief matter of time I had passed through some 60+ bombers.

I was in a relatively secure position – in between the bombers, where I could not be fired at without the gunners risking hitting one of their own bombers. Out of ammunition and over-excited, I decided to ram one! I moved into an oblique attack on a B-24. I could feel the eddies from the slipstream. My aircraft was thrown off balance and I missed my intended victim by only a few metres. Then the sky

Feldwebel Oscar Bösch of 14.(*Sturm*)/JG 3 rests his right foot in the fuselage step aperture of his Fw 190A-8/R2 'Black 14' at Schongau in August 1944 as he attends to what appears to be his parachute harness. The armoured cockpit side panel and armoured glass canopy panel are clearly visible. (Author's Collection courtesy of Oscar Bösch)

became clear in front of me. Looking around, I could see no bombers, only some kind of hell of fire. My Focke-Wulf vibrated as shots hit home, and I am sure that the lateral armour plating saved my life. Pushing my stick forward, regardless of the terrific negative G forces, I was now in a straight dive at 1000km/h, engulfed in bullets that were hitting me. Without wasting time, I undid my harness and ejected the canopy. A freezing wind snatched me from my seat. I felt terrified during my free-fall of 6000m as I waited to pass through the clouds before opening my parachute. I landed at Goslar, in the Harz. I was lucky to have been only lightly wounded in the head by some shrapnel and slightly burned on the face from my fall in the freezing air because my parachute had been pierced many times by bullets!

USAAF Intelligence later reported:

The B-24s attacking Brunswick were strongly attacked in the target area. Some mass attacks were made, but the majority of passes were made by groups of four to eight, head-on, level, and slightly high out of the sun. The formation was subjected to fierce fighter opposition in the Nienburg area, when nearing Brunswick, without escort. About 75 enemy aircraft, mostly Fw 190s, attacked in a square block formation, massing and assaulting from the nose. These pilots were experienced and viciously aggressive, pressing so closely that in one instance a bomber was destroyed by collision with an enemy fighter.

Feldwebel Bösch was accredited with a B-24 *Herausschuss* following this operation. Although IV.(*Sturm*)/JG 3's total claims amounted to 19 *Abschüsse* and *Herausschüsse*, only 11 B-24s were lost in total, with a further seven written off after returning to base severely damaged.

In mid-May 1944 Major von Kornatzki was ordered to set up II.(*Sturm*)/JG 4 at Salzwedel and Welzow. Formed around a solid core of pilots from *Sturmstaffel* 1, the *Gruppe* had to wait until late July to receive its first Fw 190A-8/R2. For most of the summer its personnel underwent conversion and tactical training.

At the end of May a third *Sturmgruppe* had also begun forming up at Rheine when 4. and 5. *Staffeln* of the single-seat *Wilde Sau* nightfighter *Gruppe*

This aircraft is believed to be an Fw 190A-8/R2 assigned to 8.(*Sturm*)/JG 300 at Löbnitz in the autumn of 1944. The rear fuselage *Geschwader* identification band was in red. (EN Archive)

II./JG 300 commenced conversion to the day fighter role under Major Kurd Peters alongside I. and III./JG 300. II./JG 300 took delivery of Fw 190A-8/R2s, while I. and III. *Gruppen* retained their Bf 109s for the escort role. Within II./JG 300, Peters was able to draw on a number of experienced combat pilots, and the new *Sturmgruppe* was designated II.(*Sturm*)/JG 300 in July 1944. By 4 August, the conversion and training of the unit as a *Sturmgruppe* was complete.

Meanwhile, since the late summer of 1943, several Luftwaffe fighter and *Zerstörer* units had deployed the underwing W.Gr.21 air-to-air mortar, which had been adapted from an army weapon. A number of Fw 190 and Bf 109 units had one of the 1.3m-long tubes, known as 'stovepipes', suspended beneath each wing of their aircraft.

The tactical value of dispersing a bomber *Pulk* had been recognised so that defensive fire could be weakened and confusion caused within an enemy formation to enable single, isolated bombers to be targeted more easily. At that point, the fighters could engage more closely and use their cannon and machine guns to bring bombers down. In such circumstances, the 21cm spin-stabilised mortar shells were usually fired into the front of an enemy formation from ranges up to 400m. However, as one Luftwaffe pilot noted, 'The closer to the target you were, so the greater the blast and the success of the weapon.'

Operational success was debatable, but in February 1944 trials commenced with a rearward-firing version of the mortar. The intention was that a pilot would fire the mortar, known as the *Krebsgerät* (Crab Device), after he had made a firing pass using forward armament against a bomber formation and was in the process of passing through the enemy *Pulk*. The fuse would be set to detonate at 1.5–2 seconds after the weapon was fired, giving sufficient time for the carrying fighter to fly ahead and clear. There was a plan to make the tube jettisonable after firing, but it is not thought this was ever followed through. It was hoped that a rearward-firing mortar would achieve surprise in the manner of a 'Parthian shot'.

In May 1944, Generalmajor Galland ordered that 20 Fw 190A-8s were to be fitted with the *Krebsgerät*, and by 15 July it was planned to have 60 such devices ready for installation into Fw 190s, with one tube mounted below the fuselage centreline between the wings. The aircraft and pilots of 12.(*Sturm*)/JG 3 were selected as 'guinea pigs' and despatched to Barth on the Baltic coast. Ultimately, just four of the *Staffel*'s aircraft were installed with a form of the *Krebsgerät*, but they proved unreliable mechanically. The additional armour already added to

Armourers load a W.Gr.21 air-to-air mortar shell into a firing tube fitted beneath the wing of an Fw 190A-8/R6 in the summer of 1944. Despite a direct hit from a 21cm mortar shell on a bomber being devastating, and just the blast effect being sufficient to break up a bomber formation, results were debatable because *Jagdwaffe* pilots tended to fire the mortar from too great a range. (EN Archive)

the unit's Fw 190A-8 *Sturmjäger* affected performance and at least one pilot who tested the weapon in combat, Unteroffizier Willi Unger, reported that the *Krebsgerät* simply caused a further deterioration in the fighter's speed and manoeuvrability. By late September trials seem to have petered out.

On 7 July the Eighth Air Force sent 939 B-17s and B-24s escorted by more than 650 fighters to attack a range of aircraft and synthetic oil plants in central Germany. At 0935 hrs, as the Liberators of the 492nd BG approached Oschersleben from the west, a *Gefechtsverband* led by Major Walther Dahl, comprising 44 Fw 190A-8s of Hauptmann Wilhelm Moritz's IV.(*Sturm*)/JG 3 from Illesheim, escorted by Bf 109G-10s from I. and III./JG 300, evaded the fighter escort and closed in on the 492nd's Low Squadron.

Initially, it had been planned to make a frontal attack against the bombers, but this was changed to a rear attack, made at 0940 hrs, 5600m over Oschersleben. Despite the massed defensive fire, the Fw 190s spread across the sky line abreast in a formidable broad front and closed to 100m before opening fire. It took the *Sturmjäger* about a minute to shoot down 11 Liberators (an entire squadron), and when the B-24s of the 2nd BD returned home, 28 of their number had been lost, most of them to the

An Fw 190 dives below a B-17 streaming flames from its port wing fuel tank during a USAAF raid on Oschersleben. It is possible that the American bomber is a lone 'straggler', having already been forced away from the protection of its 'box' formation. (EN Archive)

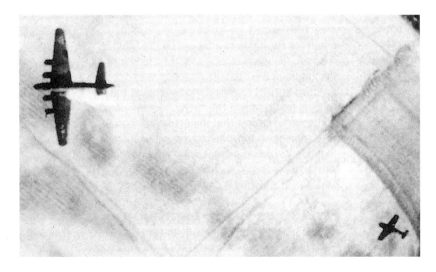

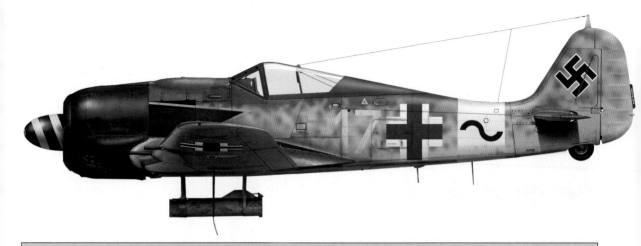

Fw 190A-8/R2 KREBSGERÄT

Fw 190A-8/R2 'Yellow 17' fitted with a rear-firing *Krebsgerät* 21cm mortar and flown by Unteroffizier Willi Unger of 12.*(Sturm)*/JG 3 during trials with the weapon from Barth in May 1944. The intention was that a pilot would make a frontal attack against a bomber *Pulk*, and as he passed overhead, would fire the mortar. The weight of the device adversely affected the Fw 190's speed and manoeuvrability, and posed a risk to other Luftwaffe fighters following behind. The *Krebsgerät* was quickly abandoned.

Sturmgruppe, which had had nine of its own aircraft destroyed in the attack. Altogether, the Eighth Air Force lost 37 heavy bombers, with another 390 damaged during the day's raid.

Prominent in the attack was Leutnant Werner Gerth, *Staffelkapitän* of 11.*(Sturm)*/JG 3 (later 14.*(Sturm)*/JG 3) who claimed his 13th and 14th victories within one minute. He would shoot down five *Viermots* during the month. Of his 27 confirmed victories, 22 were four-engined, several of them multiple victories scored in one day. Gerth's Fw 190A-8/R2 was hit by defensive fire from a B-17 over Halle on 2 November 1944 and he bailed out, but his parachute failed to open and he was killed. Gerth had been shot down 12 times previously and survived. He received a posthumous German Cross in Gold on 1 January 1945 and was promoted to Hauptmann.

Also shooting down a bomber at 0942 hrs – exactly the same moment as Gerth – was Unteroffizier Willi Unger of 12.*(Sturm)*/JG 3, whose path to becoming a *Sturm* pilot is described in Chapter 3. He reported:

I opened fire from 600m on a Liberator in the middle of the formation, and after the first burst the right wing and both right engines began to burn. With further continuous fire up to 350m range, the enemy machine veered to the right. A real fireball wrapped around the fuselage as well as the right wing, the machine tilted further to the right and immediately the enemy machine burned up. I could not see the ground impact as I went to approach a second Liberator, which I attacked and shot down.

Indeed, as Unger recorded:

During a *Sturm* attack on a Liberator *Pulk* of some 25 machines, I was able to fire at a second Liberator immediately after my first shoot-down, flying in the

Unteroffizier Willi Unger, an accomplished *Sturmgruppe* pilot of 12.*(Sturm)*/JG 3, sits on the cockpit sill of his Fw 190A-8/R2 'Yellow 17' at Barth in May 1944. The aircraft has a rearward-firing 21cm mortar tube suspended beneath its fuselage, as does the Fw 190A-8/R2 behind it. The *Krebsgerät* was to be fired back at a bomber formation once the fighter had passed through it following a gunnery attack. The weapon was a failure, and unlike the standard forward-firing underwing mortars, it was not used in significant numbers. The first 21 of Willi Unger's 24 confirmed victories were four-engined bombers. He was awarded the Knight's Cross on 23 October 1944. (Author's Collection courtesy of Willi Unger)

right half of the *Pulk*. Because of my alignment it was possible to attack the second Liberator. From about 300m, I opened continuous fire up to 100m. The hits went into the centre fuselage and tail assembly. The rear gunner was hit and pieces flew away from the tail unit. The Liberator immediately went into a downwards spiral to the right. As I made my exit past the enemy machine, two to four parachutes opened.

The two Liberators hit the ground near Oschersleben at 0942 and 0943 hrs. Like Gerth, Unger had scored his 10th and 11th victories within one minute.

0935 hrs, 7 JULY 1944

OSCHERSLEBEN

1 With the Bf 109G-10s from I. and III./JG 300 as top cover, 44 Fw 190A-8s of Hauptmann Wilhelm Moritz's IV.*(Sturm)*/JG 3 intercept the B-24s of the low squadron of the 492nd BG as they approach Oschersleben from the west.

2 Despite the massed defensive fire from the bombers, the Fw 190 pilots spread across the sky line abreast in a formidable broad front and close to 100m before opening fire.

3 In around a minute, the *Gefechtsverband* shoot down 11 Liberators – an entire squadron. However, nine aircraft from the *Sturmgruppe* are also lost in the attack.

4 Unteroffizier Willi Unger of 12.*(Sturm)*/JG 3 opens fire from 600m at a Liberator in the centre of the formation. After his initial burst, the bomber's right wing and both right engines begin to burn. As Unger closes in to 350m, firing continuously, the B-24 veers to the right. Wrapped in flames, the Liberator banks further to the right and goes down.

5 Unger then rolls to the left and engages a second B-24, raking its fuselage and tail.

6 As Unger flashes past, the Liberator lurches over and also goes down. Four crewmen manage to bail out.

FOLLOWING PAGES

Feldwebel Hans Schäfer, who flew with 10.(*Sturm*) and 13.(*Sturm*)/JG 3, is wearing a flying jacket decorated with the 'whites of the eyes' insignia on the left breast denoting that he was an experienced *Sturmgruppe* pilot. Schäfer claimed as many as 27 enemy aircraft shot down, of which eight were *Viermots*. (EN Archive)

Despite heavy losses, IV.(*Sturm*)/JG 3 moved to Schongau, near the Austrian border, at the end of July in order to oppose Fifteenth Air Force attacks originating from Italy. On 3 August, the Fifteenth sent its B-17s and B-24s to bomb aircraft and steel factories at Friedrichshafen and chemical plants and the marshalling yards at Immenstadt, but by this time the entire *Gruppe* had only 16 aircraft and could put up only four *Schwärme*. The *Schwarm* from 12.(*Sturm*)/JG 3 was led by Feldwebel Unger, with Unteroffiziere Hermann Christ, Hans-Joachim Scholz and Heinz Zimkeit. When the *Gruppe* took off to intercept the bombers that had raided Friedrichshafen, the raiders were returning to Italy, and as Unger later recalled:

Our attack was directed at a bomber unit that had bombed Friedrichshafen and was flying over the Alps to Italy. The attack took place at 1130 hrs at an altitude of 6500m over the Lechtaler Alps. We shot down six Liberators, but during our attack the American escorts rushed at us from behind. As a result we lost eight Fw 190s to escort fighters and defensive fire from the bombers. Six German pilots met their deaths, but two were able to bail out, landing high up in the Alps. Of my flight – four aircraft – only one machine made it back home. Two comrades were killed [Scholz and Zimkeit]. I myself was hit in the engine by fire from a tail gun. My windshield went black with oil and I couldn't see a thing. I was saved by my parachute and landed with a thump some 2000m up in the mountains. Fragments of my machine still lie scattered today at another spot up in the mountains. Of the six dead fighter pilots, two are still recorded as missing. Sixty-seven people were killed by bombs in Friedrichshafen, among them 22 teenage Flak gun helpers. I took part in greater air battles over Germany, but for me this was the most dramatic.

During the attack, Unger shot down a Liberator for his 15th victory. Christ and Scholz also each shot down a bomber, and in total IV.(*Sturm*)/JG 3 accounted for 19 B-24s either shot down or classified as *Herausschuss*, but had five pilots killed and one wounded. Unger walked 16km to the nearest village, where he found a car and arrived back at Schongau at midnight.

On 15 August II.(*Sturm*)/JG 300 received its baptism of fire. The Eighth Air Force used the perfect summer weather to despatch a force of nearly 900 B-17s and B-24s to bomb a range of airfield targets across Germany. At Bad Wörishofen, the *Kommodore* of JG 300, Oberstleutnant Walther Dahl, placed his 100 or so available fighters on readiness and drew up plans for a *Gefechtsverband* comprising the *Geschwaderstabsschwarm* and I./JG 300 (equipped with Bf 109G-10s and G-14s in the high-altitude escort role) at Bad Wörishofen, II.(*Sturm*)/JG 300 at Holzkirchen and IV.(*Sturm*)/JG 3 at Schongau.

Within two hours Dahl was airborne, accompanied by the 30 Bf 109s of I./JG 300 as escort. The formation headed south to Augsburg, where it made a textbook rendezvous with the 30 Fw 190s of the two *Sturmgruppen* just

after 1000 hrs. Under radio silence at 7000m, and with Dahl at the head of a great wedge-shaped battle formation, the German fighters turned towards Frankfurt, some 260km away. IV.(*Sturm*)/JG 3's Fw 190s were flying in two stacked-down *Sturmkeil*.

Thirty minutes later, the fighter controllers ordered a change in course to Trier, 150km further west. After one hour of flying in slowly deteriorating weather, the *Gefechtsverband* finally sighted three *Pulks* of 60–80 B-17s west of the Mosel River. Just before 1145 hrs, Dahl manoeuvred his *Angriffskeil* for an attack from the rear, with Moritz's IV.(*Sturm*)/JG 3 assigned to the *Pulk* flying to his left and II.(*Sturm*)/JG 300, led by 5. *Staffel* commander Leutnant Klaus Bretschneider, on the right. Dahl and the *Stabsschwarm* would tackle the centre *Pulk*.

Within sight of the enemy bomber formation and some 90–150 above and 900–1500m behind it, the *Sturmgruppe* dropped its external tanks, then re-formed from its Vee formation into its line abreast *Angriffsformation* or *Breitkeil*. This was carried out by climbing where necessary and fanning out into a slightly swept-back line abreast formation of usually more than 20 fighters, either level with or slightly above the enemy, with the commander of the *Gruppe* and his deputy flying at its apex.

In one pass, the combined JG 3/JG 300 attack shot down or 'cut out' 13 B-17s of the 303rd BG near Trier. Dahl claimed two Flying Fortresses, while another bomber fell to Berliner Klaus Bretschneider, who would go on to claim a total of 17 *Viermots*, including three in one day on 7 October, before being shot down and killed by a P-51 while flying against bombers near Kassel on 24 December. Bretschneider's comrade Feldwebel Konrad Bauer also claimed a B-17 for his 13th bomber. 'Pitt' Bauer was a ferocious attack pilot who had shot down three B-24s of the Fifteenth Air Force over Hungary on 27 July 1944. He finally accounted for 14 four-engined bombers out of a total of 39 victories. Bauer, who was shot down seven times and lost two fingers from his right hand while in combat with P-51s, received the Knight's Cross on 31 October 1944.

Officers of IV.(*Sturm*)/JG 3 watch activity at Illesheim in July 1944. Joining them at far right is Major Walther Dahl, the *Kommodore* of JG 300. To his right is Hauptmann Wilhelm Moritz, *Kommandeur* of IV.(*Sturm*)/JG 3, while second from left is Oberleutnant Ekkehard Tichy, who would be appointed *Staffelkapitän* of 10.(*Sturm*)/JG 3 in August 1944, only to be killed in action on the 16th of that same month. In the background is Fw 190A-8 'Black 13', which has been fitted with additional side armour. During the summer of 1944, this aircraft was flown by Leutnant Werner Gerth of 11.(*Sturm*)/JG 3, who claimed a total of 27 victories (at least 16 are believed to have been B-17s) prior to his death in combat on 2 November 1944. (EN Archive)

A member of the groundcrew assists a pilot of JG 300 with his parachute on the wing of what is believed to be Fw 190A-8 'Blue 13', flown by the *Geschwaderkommodore*, Major Walther Dahl. The pilot does not appear to be Dahl, however, so this was probably a 'photo opportunity' taken shortly after returning from a sortie (it was considered an ill omen to photograph a pilot just before a mission). The aircraft carries Dahl's personal emblem – a B-17 framed within the crosshairs of a gunsight. (EN Archive)

Also victorious on 15 August was Oberleutnant Ekkehard Tichy from the Sudetenland, *Kapitän* of 13.*(Sturm)*/JG 3, who shot down a B-17. Although he had been wounded in one of his eyes during a clash with escort fighters on 18 March 1944 while with 9./JG 3, Tichy returned to duty and subsequently shot down eight *Viermots*. On 16 August he downed his 25th and final victory – another B-17, with which he collided, possibly as a result of his impaired vision. Tichy was killed. He was posthumously awarded the Knight's Cross.

Just under a month later, on 11 September, Oberstleutnant von Kornatzki's II.*(Sturm)*/JG 4 flew one of its most successful operations against the bombers since its formation in the summer. That day, the Eighth Air Force launched 1016 heavy bombers from all three of its Bomb Divisions, escorted by 411 fighters, against eight synthetic oil plants, marshalling yards and an ordnance depot in central Germany. At 1030 hrs, II.*(Sturm)*/JG 4, with III./JG 4 providing its escort, received the *Startbefehl* (start command) and more than 60 Fw 190s and Bf 109s took off from Welzow and Alteno to form part of a *Gefechtsverband* which would fall under the tactical control of Major Günther Specht and the *Geschwaderstab* of JG 11. With accurate guidance from the ground, the two *Gruppen* of JG 4 were vectored towards Chemnitz. At 1210 hrs the unit had its first sighting of the bombers, although by this time aircraft from IV.*(Sturm)*/JG 3 and II.*(Sturm)*/JG 300 were already engaging the 1st BD and its escort. JG 4 would take on the 3rd BD southwest of Chemnitz.

Minutes later, at about 1210 hrs, and at an altitude of 8000–9000m, with the Allied fighter escort already occupied, II.*(Sturm)*/JG 4 went to work on the bombers to such effect that 15 pilots, including Hauptmanns Manfred Köpcke, *Staffelkapitän* of 6.*(Sturm)*/JG 4, and Erich Jugel, *Kapitän* of 5.*(Sturm)*/JG 4, each claimed a B-17 either shot down or a *Herausschuss* within three minutes. But the attack had not been without cost. 5. *Staffel* lost three pilots, 6. *Staffel* suffered five casualties and 7.*(Sturm)*/JG 4 lost three, all some 20km south of Chemnitz.

At 1219 hrs, the Fw 190s of 8.*(Sturm)*/JG 4, which had formed a high rear escort element for the *Sturmgruppe* in case the Bf 109s of III./JG 4 were not able to offer sufficient protection, also waded in from the rear of the *Pulk* at around 8000m. However, due to intervention by American fighters, their formation was not as tight as it should have been. Nevertheless, eight claims were made by eight pilots including the *Staffelkapitän*, Hauptmann Gerhard Schroeder. Leutnant Alfred Rausch rammed a B-17 with his Fw 190 A-8/R2 'Blue 16' over Reitzenhain/Komotau and was killed in the process.

By the end of the action, II.(*Sturm*)/JG 4 had claimed 16 Flying Fortresses shot down, with a further seven classified as *Herausschuss*, while III./JG 4 claimed nine B-17s destroyed with three *Herausschüsse*, plus four escort fighters. However, these victories came at a heavy price, with II. *Gruppe* reporting 12 pilots lost, together with nine from III. *Gruppe*. The cost in aircraft was high too – JG 4 estimated that as a result of this operation, between a third and a half of its machines needed repair. Twenty-three Fw 190s were classified as 60–100 per cent damaged, with 27 Bf 109s reported at the same level. For the USAAF, the cost was equally high with 40 heavy bombers and 17 fighters lost during the raid.

The next day, 12 September, JG 4 was to receive a blow when Oberstleutnant von Kornatzki, the popular tactician and 'father' of the *Sturm* concept, was killed after an engagement with American bombers. During the late morning he had shot down a B-17 at 8000m some 30km west of Magdeburg during another USAAF attack on the oil plants, but his aircraft was damaged by the bombers' defensive fire. Pursued by an American escort fighter, von Kornatzki attempted to make an emergency landing, only for his Fw 190A-8 to crash into power lines at Zilly, near Halberstadt. Von Kornatzki's loss was simultaneous to, and symbolic of, the atrophy facing the *Sturmjäger* in the face of an ever-strengthening enemy.

1145 hrs, 15 AUGUST 1944

KOBLENZ

1 North of Augsburg, a mixed formation of Fw 190s from II.(*Sturm*)/JG 300 and IV.(*Sturm*)/JG 3, together with their escorting Bf 109Gs, join into one large attack force heading for a formation of 900 B-17s bound for targets in western and southern Germany. After an hour of flying, and in slowly deteriorating weather, the *Gefechtsverband* finally sights three *Pulks* of 60–80 Flying Fortresses of the 1st BD just west of the Mosel River.

2 Just before 1145 hrs, Oberstleutnant Walther Dahl, *Kommodore* of JG 300, manoeuvres his *Angriffskeil* for a classic attack from the rear, with Hauptmann Wilhelm Moritz's IV.(*Sturm*)/JG 3 assigned to the *Pulk* flying to his left and Leutnant Klaus Bretschneider's II.(*Sturm*)/JG 300 to the *Pulk* on the right. Dahl and the *Stabsschwarm* will tackle the centre *Pulk*.

3 Dahl lines up on a B-17 from the 303rd BG flying to the left of his selected group and commences firing at 300m, continuing to close in. He see his rounds striking home in the fuselage and right wing root, and debris flying away. A few seconds later, the bomber veers to the left, with flames and smoke from the right wing trailing over the fuselage. Three crewmen bail out. As Dahl passes through the formation, the B-17's right wing breaks away and the aircraft noses downwards.

4 At the same time, 25 Fw 190s from Dahl's *Gefechtsverband* attack the low squadron aircraft from the 303rd BG's 358th and 427th BSs. Nine of the 13 bombers in the low squadron are shot down.

5 Dahl orders his formation to re-form and make a second attack. Selecting a second *Viermot*, Dahl once again closes in from 200m to 80m, firing with machine guns and cannon. The port inboard engine of his foe starts to burn and the B-17 begins to drop away from the formation. Dahl hurriedly counts five parachutes, just as the P-51D escort from the 383rd FS/364th FG arrives. With fuel now low, the *Sturmjäger* disengage and turn for the nearest airfields cleared for their arrival, leaving the Bf 109s to take on the Mustangs.

FOLLOWING PAGES

AFTERMATH

By the autumn of 1944, the Luftwaffe daylight fighter force defending the German homeland – the *Reichsverteidigung* – was caught in the effects of a perfect storm. Not only did its commanders and pilots have to fight a more powerful external enemy, but increasingly there was an enemy within; his name was Hermann Göring. From mid-1944 Göring, whose reputation, along with that of the Luftwaffe, in the eyes of Hitler was tarnished and withered, refused to accept any reasoning or realities associated with the air war over the Reich. His priority was to salvage his prestige. As far as he was concerned his fighter formations were poorly led. At a meeting of his *Reichsverteidigung* commanders at the headquarters of *Luftflotte Reich* at Berlin-Wannsee on 26 October he allegedly exclaimed:

> I want 500 B-17s brought down next time or I'll have you transferred to the infantry! The Allies know how to put up a good show at fighter protection – use them as an example!

This temperament overlooked certain realities which the Reichsmarschall perhaps preferred not to see. To place this in context, less than a week after the meeting in Berlin, the commander of *Luftflotte Reich*, Generaloberst Hans-Jürgen Stumpff, penned a new order to his regional airfield commands:

> The fuel situation makes further restriction of flying operations essential. I therefore issue the following orders:

Leutnant Klaus Bretschneider of 5.(*Sturm*)/JG 300 seated at the controls to his Fw 190A-8/R2 Wk-Nr 682204 'Red 1' *Rauhbautz VII* at Löbnitz. At the time of his death in action on 24 December 1944, Bretschneider had lodged claims for at least 30 enemy aircraft destroyed, of which 26 were four-engined bombers, while flying the Fw 190A, and there were further probables. He was awarded the Knights Cross on 18 November 1944. Standing on the wing of the Focke-Wulf is fellow Knight's Cross-holder and *Staffel* comrade Oberfeldwebel Konrad Bauer, who claimed 38 victories, including 13 four-engined bombers. (EN Archive)

1. A sortie is justifiable only if weather reports and the available tactical information promise success. Those responsible for operations must bear this in mind when issuing operational orders.

2. Training flights within units are prohibited until further notice unless specific quotas are issued for the purpose. My approval is required for exceptions to this rule.

3. No flights may be undertaken except for operational transfer, test and transport purposes.

Fw 190s of II.(*Sturm*)/JG 300 at readiness at Finsterwalde in the autumn of 1944. All the aircraft have been fitted with 300-litre drop tanks. Rather than enabling long-range over-water flights, such tanks were often fitted to give range to units assembling from distances into *Gefechtsverbände*, or being brought into a battle area by divisional controls from distant parts of the Reich. (EN Archive)

Within weeks of Stumpff's diktat, however, the dichotomous nature of the *Reichsverteidigung* became highly evident. On 1 January 1945, 143 German pilots were killed or reported missing. Amongst their number were three *Geschwaderkommodore*, five *Gruppenkommandeure* and 14 *Staffelkapitäne*, with a further 21 pilots wounded and 70 taken prisoner, as a result of the over-ambitious surprise attack on Allied tactical airfields across northwest Europe in what was named Operation *Bodenplatte*. On 7 April 1945, the ill-fated *Sonderkommando Elbe* mission flown against a USAAF raid by ideologically motivated but generally inexperienced young pilots given authority to ram enemy bombers with their Bf 109s resulted in the deaths of some 24 pilots and the loss of 45 Bf 109s for the destruction of around 12 B-17s.

These tactical catastrophes should be set against a battle which was changing technologically. The appearance of the high-performance American P-51

Dangerous skies – this Fw 190 was caught by the gun camera of a pursuing USAAF fighter over northwest Europe. (EN Archive)

Mustang and British Tempest V fighters had to be contested by the new 'long-nosed' and nimble Fw 190D-9, which, necessarily, could not be burdened by heavy armour like its Fw 190A-6, A-7 and A-8 'predecessors'.

Luftwaffe commanders also feared the arrival of the formidable B-29 Superfortress four-engined heavy bomber which, it was believed, would replace the USAAF's B-17s and B-24s during 1945. The high-altitude B-29, which was already in operation in the Far East, had a greater bomb-load capacity than the B-17. The interim German response to this impending threat was Kurt Tank's superlative Ta 152.

Salvation also came in the form of the revolutionary Me 262 jet- and Me 163 rocket-powered interceptors which possessed the superior speed required to out-fly the latest Allied fighter types, as well as the ability to deliver modern stand-off weapons such as the DWM 55mm R4M and Ruhrstahl X4 air-to-air rockets.

Close-range attacks, mounted by slow, heavily armoured fighters, were no longer viable. To combat the new generation of American heavy bombers effectively, the new generation of Luftwaffe fighters needed speed, altitude and accurate stand-off weaponry. By 1945, the *Jagdwaffe* had all of these things, but never enough of them, never enough pilots, never enough fuel and never enough time.

SELECTED SOURCES

Caldwell, Donald and Muller, Richard, *The Luftwaffe Over Germany – Defense of the Reich* (Greenhill Books, London, 2007)

Carlsen, Sven and Meyer, Michael, *Die Flugzeugführer-Ausbildung Der Deutschen Luftwaffe 1935–1945 Band II* (Heinz Nickel Verlag, Zweibrücken, 2000)

Craven, W. F. and Cate, J. L., *The Army Air Forces in World War II, Volume I – Plans and Early Operations (January 1939 to August 1942)* (The University of Chicago Press, Chicago, 1948)

Forsyth, Robert, *Jagdwaffe – Defending the Reich 1943–1944* (Classic Publications, Hersham, 2004)

Forsyth, Robert, *Jagdwaffe – Defending The Reich 1944–1945* (Classic Publications, Hersham, 2005)

Freeman, Roger A., *Mighty Eighth War Manual* (Janes, London, 1984)

Lorant, Jean-Yves and Goyat, Richard, *Jagdgeschwader 300 'Wilde Sau' Volume One – June 1943–September 1944* (Eagle Editions, Hamilton, 2005)

McFarland, Stephen L. and Phillips Newton, Wesley, *To Command the Sky – The Battle for Air Superiority over Germany, 1942–1944* (Smithsonian Institution Press, Washington, 1991)

Mombeek, Eric, *Defending The Reich – The History of Jagdgeschwader 1 'Oesau'* (JAC Publications, Norwich, 1992)

Mombeek, Eric, *Defenders of the Reich – Jagdgeschwader 1 – Volume Three 1944–1945* (Classic Publications, Hersham, 2003)

Mombeek, Eric with Forsyth, Robert and Creek, Eddie J., *Sturmstaffel 1 – Reich Defence 1943–1944 The War Diary* (Classic Publications, Crowborough, 1999)

Prien, Jochen, *IV./Jagdgeschwader 3 – Chronik Einer Jagdgruppe 1943–1945* (Struve-Druck, Eutin, undated)

Prien, Jochen and Rodeike, Peter, *Jagdgeschwader 1 Und 11 – Teil 2 1944* (Struve-Druck, Eutin, undated)

INDEX

Page numbers in **bold** refer to illustrations. Some caption locators are in brackets.

aerial combat 4–7, **5**, 11–13, 33–34, 42
  battle readiness 38–39
  close range tactics 35–36, **37**, 38, 78
  frontal attacks 34–35, **35**, **37**, 40, 43–44, 54, 58
  ramming 36, 45, **60–61** (59), 62–63, 72, 77
  rear attacks 34, 35, 36, 40, 42, **48**, 65–66
aircraft (other than Fw 190)
  B-17 Flying Fortress 4, 5, **5**, 6–7, 10, **10**, 11, 33, **34**, **35**, **36**, **39**, 42, 43–44, 50–51, 53, 54, 58, **65**, 70, 71–72, **74–75** (73)
  B-17F 42-3040 *MISS OUACHITA* **47**
  B-17F 42-3352 *Virgin's Delight* **12**
  B-17F 42-30181 *HERKY JERKY II* 44–45
  B-17G 42-31432 *My Darling Also* 51
  B-17G 42-31924 *OL' DOG* **56–57** (55)
  B-24 Liberator 4, **8**, 33–34, 42, 45–46, **52**, 54–55, 58, **60–61** (59), 62–63, 65–66, 66–67, **68–69** (67), 70, 71–72
  B-29 Superfortress 78
  Bf 109: **13**, 19, **19**, 32, 38
  Bf 110: 11
  Me 262: 78
  Me 263: 78
  Me 410: 11
  numbers of 15
  P-38 Lightening 42
  P-47 Thunderbolt 10, **10**, 11, 42
  P-51 Mustang 10, 13–14, 31, **39**, 48–49, 50, 53, 77–78
airfields 9, **14**, 15, 21, 39, 52, 53–54, 70–71, 77
armour plating and glass 28–29, 31, 32, **32**, **49**, **55**, 64–65, **71**
Arnold, Lt Gen Henry 'Hap' 15

Bacsila, Maj Erwin **49**
Bär, Maj Heinz 46–47, **47**, 54, 59, 62
Bauer, OFw Konrad 71, **76**
Berlin 48–52, 62
bombing raids *see* combat details
Bösch, Fw Oscar 23, 23, 31, 40, 46, **60–61** (59), 62–63, **63**
Braunschweig 45, 52–53, 54, 62
Bretschneider, Lt Klaus 71, **74–75** (73), **76**
Brunner, Fw Wolfgang 54–55
Buchholz, Lt Günther 6

cameras 32
casualties and losses 7, 10, 11, 12–13, 15, 42, 44, 45, 52, 58, 62, 65–66, 70, 73, 77
Christ, Hermann 70
combat details 41–75, 58
  aftermath 76–78
  airfield raids, 8 April 1944: 54–55
  aviation/industrial targets, 11 January 1944: 42–44
  Berlin and Braunschweig, 8 May 1944: **60–61** (59), 62–63
  'Big-B' missions 48–52
  Braunschweig and Hannover raids 45–46
  combat over Fallersleben 59, 62
  events of 15 August 1944: **74–75** (73)
  Friedrichshafen and Immenstadt raids, 3 August 1944: 70
  Kiel attack 41–42
  Leipzig-Mockau, Halberstadt and Regensburg raids 47–48
  Münster raid, 23 March 1944: 52–53
  oil plants raid, 7 July 1944: 65–67, **68–69** (67)
  raids of 11 September 1944: 72
  raids of 15 August 1944: 70–72
combat planning and preparation 11–13, 14–16, **14**, 17–23
  tactics 33–40, **37**

Dahl, Maj Walther 65, 70–71, **71**, **72**, **74–75** (73)
Dost, Lt Gerhard 51
drop tanks 24, 29, 30, 31, 39, **40**, 77

Eaker, Brig Gen Ira C. 9–10
Eder, OLt Georg-Peter 4, 5, **6**, 54, 59, 62
engines 25, 29, **29**, 30
Engleder, ObLt Rudolf 12, 13

Födisch, OFw Lothar 55
formation flying **9**, 10, **10**, 33, 36, **37**, 38–39, 71
Frankfurt 11–12, 44
Franz, Lt Richard 16, 26–27, 36, 38, 45, 49–50, 55, 58
Frey, Lt Hugo 52
friendly fire **60–61** (59), 62
Fuchs, Fw Heinz 42
fuel 24, 31, 76–77
fuselage 20, 30, 31, 46, 51
Fw 190: 12–13, **15**, 33, 40, 44–45, **60–61** (59), **65**, **74–75** (73), 77, 78
  airframe 25
  assembly 26
  Fw 190A-5 WkNr 410011 GG+MV 20
  Fw 190A-6: 24, **26**, 41, **46**, **49**
  Fw 190A-6/R1: 25–27
  Fw 190A-6/R2: 27–28, 29
  Fw 190A-6/R3: 28
  Fw 190A-6/R4: 29
  Fw 190A-6/R6: 28
  Fw 190A-7: 4–5, 7, 23, 29, **41**, 43, **45**, 51, 53
  Fw 190A-7 Wk-Nr 642545 WQ+VC 29
  Fw 190A-8: 4–5, 6–7, **21**, 30, **30**, 31–32, **32**, 55, **56–57** (55), **63**, 65, **68–69** (67), **71**, 72
  Fw 190A-8/R2: 27, **64**, 66, **76**
  Fw 190A-8/R2 Krebsgerät 66
  Fw 190A-8/R2 'Yellow 17' **67**
  Fw190D-9: 78
  markings and identification **7**, **41**, **43**, **45**, **72**
  weight 26–27

Galland, GenMaj Adolf 10, **11**, 16, 34, 36, 64
Galland, Maj Wilhelm-Ferdinand 'Wutz' 10
Gerth, Lt Walter 52, 58, 66, **71**
Göring, Hermann 11, 12, 76
Grislawski, Hptm Alfred 44–45, **45**
ground crew **13**, **21**, **41**, **51**, **53**, **72**

Hackl, Maj Anton 39–40
Hitler, Adolf **11**, 76

Jeschonnek, Gen Hans 11
Jugel, Hptm Erich 72

Keitel, GFM Wilhelm 11
Kiel 41–42
Knoblauch, Uffz Christian 6–7
Kommandogerät (command device) 30–31
Köpcke, Hptm Manfred 72
Kreitzman, SSgt Harvey 44
Kretschmer, ObLt Wolfgang 50

Luftwaffe
  1.*Jagddivision* 4, 5
  I *Jagdkorps* 14, 21, 35, 39, 42
  Sturmstaffel 1: 16, 23, 24, 36, 38, 40, 41, 43, **43**, 44–47, 49, 50–53, 58
  I./JG 1: 12–13, **41**, 42, 43, 44–47, 50
  II./JG 1: 4–7, 11–13, 42, 43–44, 46–47, 50, 54–55, 59, 62
  III./JG 2: 33–34
  IV./JG 3: 32, 38, 40, 53, 55, 58, **60–61** (59), 62
  3./JG 11: **15**
  4./JG1: 6–7, 42
  4. *Staffel* 6
  11./JG 3: 21, 39, **56–57** (55)
  II.(*Sturm*)/JG 4: 72–73
  II.(*Sturm*)/JG 300: 64, 70–72, 72, **72**, **74–75** (73), 77
  IV.(*Sturm*)/JG 3: **68–69** (67), 70, 71–72, **71**, 72, **74–75** (73)
  8.(*Sturm*)/JG 4: 72
  12.(*Sturm*)/JG 3: 70
  order of battle 15

Marienburg plant **12**
Maximowitz, Uffz Willi 45, **46**, 51, 53
Mayer, Hptm Egon 33–34, **34**, 48, 54
Mertens, Uffz Helmut 7
Milch, GFM Erhard **11**
Moritz, Hptm Wilhelm 62, **71**, **74–75** (73)
Müller, Lt Siegfried 55, 58

Nielinger, Ofw Rudolf 19–20, **19**

Oberkommando der Luftwaffe (OKL) 35
Oesau, ObstLt Walter 42
Operation *Argument* 16, 47–48
Operation *Bodenplatte* 77
Operation *Pointblank* 16, 42–43

Peinemann, Fw Walter 46, 49
pilots **13**, **15**, 40
  insignia **70**
  morale 16
  personal experiences 23, 31, 32, 40, 62–63, 66–67, 70
  steel helmets 46
  training 14, 15, 17–21, **22**, 77
  uniform 17
Proff, Lt Helmut 6

radio equipment 25, 32
Röhrich, Uffz Kurt 51, 53, 55, 58
Rotte 40, 42

Schäfer, Fw Hans **70**
Schmid, GenMaj Josef 14, 15, 16, 21–22
Schmidt, Uffz Karl-Heinz **56–57** (55)
Scholz, Uffz Hans-Joachim 70
Schulz, Fw Adolf 6
Schweinfurt 10, 12–13
Stumpff, GenObst Hans-Jürgen 76–77

Tichy, ObLt Ekkehard **71**, 72

Ulrich, 2Lt Norman A. **56–57** (55)
Unger, OFw Willi 17–19, **17**, 20, 21, 32, 39, 65, 66–67, **66**, **67**, **68–69** (67), 70
USAAF
  Eighth Air Force 4, 8, 9, 15, 16, 38, 45, 46–47, 49, 58, 65–66, 70, 72
  Ninth Air Force 48, 58
  Fifteenth Air Force 16, 70
  VIII Bomber Command 9–10, 33, 41, 44, 49, 58
  1st Bomb Div 4, 5, 13, 42, 50, 52, 53, 54, 72, **74–75** (73)
  2nd Bomb Div 42, 48, 54, 55, 58, 62, 65–66
  3rd Bomb Div 46, 49, 54, **56–57** (55), 58, 62, 72
  post-mission reports 52, 58, 63

Vivroux, Uffz Gerhard 49, 53, 58
Von Kirchmayr, Lt Rüdiger 43–44
Von Kornatzi, Maj Hans- Günter 35–36, **35**, 52–53, 63, 72, 73

Wahlfeld, Uffz Hermann 45, 49, 51, 53
weaponry
  bombs 12
  cannon 6, **13**, 24–25, **26**, 27–28, **27**, 29, 31, 32, 49
  gunsights 29–30
  machine guns 6, **8**, 24, 25, **25**, **27**, 29, 31–32, **45**, 55
  mortars **28**, 32, 50, 64–65, **65**, **66**, **67**
  rockets 78
weather 12, 15–16
Wurl, Uffz Fritz 6

Zehart, ObLt Othmar 40, 43, 51
Zemke, Col Hubert 'Hub' 50
Zimkeit, Uffz Hans 70